ON THE HUMOR SIDE

ON THE
HUMOR SIDE

WM. M. HOLUB

THE BRUCE PUBLISHING COMPANY
New York   MILWAUKEE   Chicago

TO

John P. Mulgrew

"A Fellow of Infinite Jest"

Here's to the joke, the good old joke,
  The joke that our fathers told;
It is ready tonight and is jolly and bright
  As it was in the days of old.

When Adam was young it was on his tongue,
  And Noah got in the swim
By telling the jest as the brightest and best
  That ever happened to him.

So here's to the joke, the good old joke
  We'll hear it again tonight
Its health we will quaff; that will help us laugh,
  And treat it in manner polite.

                              — *Lew Dockstader*

Foreword

It's no joke: thousands of books, magazines, newspapers, and periodicals have been searched in order to bring you this array of little bits with the "cap and bells." They come to you with no malice in their little hearts. They are dwarfs and Snow White. So since their characters are irreproachable it is hoped that you will enjoy the party which they are about to commence for your entertainment.

As seen at a glance the jokes herein contained concern religion and kindred subjects. Special care has been used to avoid including offensive remarks toward any religion.

You, who preach sermons, or teach Sunday school, or make "brief and witty" after-dinner speeches, or pick up newspaper fillers may call this the World's Worst Joke Book — did you ever see a good one? — and if you do, kindly give your master of ceremonies credit at least for this achievement. But before you begin the presentin' of any such honors keep this thought in mind: many a joke in print that has no more apparent warmth than a lonely iceberg down in "Little America" will send an audience digging into their pockets to wipe away the "laughing tears" when repeated by a Will Rogers or that little radio dummy, Charlie McCarthy.

One of the great saints has told us in just so many words that a galaxy of funmakers like those which we are about to present, have an important place in the religious life. Says St. Teresa, "What would become of us if everyone endeavored to bury the little bit of humor and wit she has? Do not imitate those unfortunate people, who, as soon as they have acquired a little piety, put on a gloomy and peevish air, and seem to be afraid of speaking for fear that their piety will fly away."

So, now good friends, enter under this humorous Big Top to

see here gathered freaks and oddities gathered from every corner of the habitable globe, not to fiendishly gnash their teeth at you, but to make you show your teeth in wide-open laughter.

W. M. H.

Contents

ON THE HUMOR SIDE

Atheism

Henri Vignaud, for many years secretary of the American embassy at Paris, tells a story of a certain Monsieur Renaud who came to the capital as Senator from a district in the Pyrenees.

Renaud engaged a room at a hotel in Paris and paid a month's rent in advance. The proprietor asked him whether he would take a receipt.

"A receipt is unnecessary," said Renaud, "God has witnessed the payment."

"Do you believe in God?" sneered the hotelkeeper.

"Most assuredly," replied Renaud. "Don't you?"

"Not I, Monsieur."

"Ah," said Renaud, "in that case please make me out a receipt!"

※　　　※　　　※

A preacher in Ohio once came forward with the declaration that Satan was not mentioned in the Old Testament.

"Well, what of it?" asked someone of a friend who had told him of this statement.

"He claims," continued the other, with reference to the preacher, "that, as there is no mention of the devil in the Old Testament, there cannot be a devil."

"That's no proof," said the friend. "The Old Testament does not mention the Ohio Legislature, but there is one."

— *Harper's Magazine*

※　　　※　　　※

Clarence Darrow said on his seventy-ninth birthday, "I say that religion is the belief in a future life and in God. I don't believe in either."

1

To this remark, Mr. Arthur Brisbane, famous columnist made reply, "The hoptoad beside the track watching the express train go by might reasonably say: 'I don't believe in such a thing as a locomotive engineer.' "

      ⋈   ⋈   ⋈

A Scotch girl, rosy cheeked and demure, was in one corner of a compartment in a Continental train. In the corner opposite sat an atheist. The Scotch girl was reading the Bible. The atheist noticed this and after looking the girl over critically, asked whether she actually believed all she found in the Bible.

"Aye," answered she, raising her eyes to him from the page.

"Not the story of Adam and Eve?"

"Aye."

"And of Cain and Abel?"

"Aye."

"But certainly you don't believe the story of Jonah and the whale?"

The girl said she believed that, too. The atheist was puzzled.

"But how are you going to prove it? Ask Jonah when you get to heaven?"

That idea struck the girl as a good one, and she said she could prove it that way.

"Suppose he isn't there? What then? How would you prove it?"

"Ah," said the demure maiden, "then you ask him."

      ⋈   ⋈   ⋈

Here Lies an Atheist
All Dressed Up and No Place to Go.

      ⋈   ⋈   ⋈

Voltaire was one day dining with the King of Prussia in his castle at Cleves. During the repast, the French atheist, as was his wont, lost no opportunity of scoffing at religion and its votaries.

The guests listened at first in silence; but at last one of them, a stout burgomaster, filled with righteous indignation at hearing all he held most sacred thus turned into ridicule, could restrain himself no longer.

"As for me," Voltaire was saying in a sneering tone, "I would sell my place in heaven for a Prussian dollar."

"Monsieur de Voltaire," observed the burgomaster, "in Prussia we never buy costly goods without feeling sure of the owner's right to them. If you can prove your right to a place in heaven, I will buy it for the sum of ten thousand dollars."

For once the quick-witted atheist had no reply.

❈   ❈   ❈

An agnostic is one who thinks that he knows all about everything, and that other people know nothing about anything.

❈   ❈   ❈

Two men were working side by side at the shipyard. "Listen, Felix," said one, "that was an awful break ye made yesterday at Callaghan's funeral." "What do ye mane?" queried Felix. "Why," said the other, "you an' me went in to see him, an' ye no sooner took a look at him, an' ye bust out laughin'. That was no way to do at a funeral, an' hurtin' people's feelin's." "Oh! that," said Felix. "I'll tell ye why. Ye see, the day before he was kilt, him an' me was workin' together, an' he was afther tellin' me he didn't believe aither in heaven or hell, an' when I saw him I had to laugh, for there he was, all dressed up an' no place to go."

❈   ❈   ❈

It is heartening to hear Bernard Shaw speak so well of himself in these atheistic days when so many do not believe in God.

—*Israel Zangwill*

The Bible

Minister — "And how did Noah spend his time in the ark?"
Small Boy — "Fishin'."
Minister — "A very reasonable suggestion my laddie."
Small Boy (*guardedly*) — "But he wouldna catch muckle."
Minister (*surprised*) — "What makes ye think that?"
Small Boy (*knowingly*) — "Because, ye see, he had only twa wir-r-ms!"
— *London Sketch*

❈ ❈ ❈

Sunday-School Teacher — "Ernest, who defeated the Philistines?"
Ernest (*roused from daydream*) — "Dunno. I don't follow none o' them bush league teams."
— *The Passing Show* (London)

❈ ❈ ❈

"And do you know your Bible, my child?"
"Oh, yes! I know everything that's in it. Sister's young man's photo is in it, an' ma's recipe for face cream, an' a lock of my hair cut off when I was a baby, an' the ticket for Pa's watch."

❈ ❈ ❈

Mr. Van Loon cannot be charged with leaving nothing to the imagination of his readers when he tells them that the serpent "handed" Eve the fruit of the tree.
— *Boston Herald*

❈ ❈ ❈

Embarrassed Preacher (*reading the first chapter of Jonah, and making the best of the seventeenth verse*) — "And the Lord prepared a great fish to swallow up Jonah; and Jonah was in the

4

— er — a — and Jonah was in the — er — And the Lord prepared a great fish to swallow up Jonah; and Jonah was in the society of the fish three days and three nights." —*Life*

※ ※ ※

Joseph was the straightest man in the Bible because Pharaoh wanted to make a ruler of him.

※ ※ ※

William Jennings Bryan tried his hand at condensing one of the proverbs of Solomon. In a speech before the legislature of Oklahoma he said, "One proverb I have often quoted is, 'The wise man forseeth the evil and hideth himself, but the foolish pass on and are punished.' It is a great truth, and beautifully expressed, but I found it did not stick in people's minds, and so I condensed it, and it is the only effort I have ever made to improve upon a proverb and this is not an improvement, it is merely a condensation. It is not as beautiful as Solomon's proverb, but more easily remembered. It means the same thing in a condensed form. 'The wise man gets the idea into his head, the foolish man gets it in the neck.' "

※ ※ ※

No wonder Cain turned out badly, there wasn't a single book on child psychology.

※ ※ ※

Mr. Commonstock — "I sent a Bible to my boy at college and requested him to read the chapters which I had marked. Then in each of those chapters I placed a five-dollar bill."

Mr. Familyman — "Ah! a good scheme! Do you think he read them?"

Mr. Commonstock — "I guess so, for he's just mailed me the Bible asking that I mark some more chapters and return them as soon as possible." —*Puck*

Sunday-School Teacher — "Why did Adam and Eve clothe themselves after the fall?"

Bright Scholar — "Cause winter comes after fall."

— Puck

✂   ✂   ✂

Picnic parties believe that Noah had more than two ants in the ark.

— Columbia Record

✂   ✂   ✂

The Bible is great enough to survive everything, even the queer translations.

— Associated Editors (Chicago)

✂   ✂   ✂

Eye Openers — "In choosing his men," said the Sabbath-school superintendent, "Giddeon did not select those who laid aside their arms and threw themselves down to drink; he took those who watched with one eye and drank with the other."

— Philadelphia Public Ledger

✂   ✂   ✂

The Bible continues to be the world's best seller, even though no effort is made to suppress it.

— Wichita Falls Record-News

✂   ✂   ✂

Mr. Quoter — "Solomon has said, 'The race is not to the swift nor the battle to the strong.'"

Mr. Gamesport — "I suppose in his time the sporting competition was pretty crooked."

— Brooklyn Life

✂   ✂   ✂

"Who was the greatest financier ever known?"

"Noah, because he floated his stock when the world was in liquidation."

— N. Y. Press

A few months ago a preacher delivered a discourse on "Jonah" in which he is reported to have said: "When Jonah left that fish he hit the ground a-runnin', and started full tilt for Nineveh. One of the sisters looked out of her window, and saw a cloud of dust down the road, and after looking intently, said to her husband, 'I believe in my soul, yonder comes Brother Jonah!' She went to the door and hollered, 'Good morning.'"

"Good morning," answered Jonah, without turning his head.

"Where you goin' so fast, Brother Jonah?"

"Goin' to Nineveh," he replied.

"Well, stop and take dinner with us."

"Ain't got time. Three days late now."

"Oh, come in and get your dinner, Brother Jonah. We've got fish for dinner."

"Don't talk to me about fish," said Brother Jonah.

"Well, come in and have a drink of water."

"Don't talk to me about water" — and on he went a-clipping toward Nineveh. — *The United Presbyterian*

※　　　※　　　※

Teacher — "Quote a Scripture verse."

The Kid — "Judas went out into the garden and hanged himself."

Teacher — "That's fine. Quote another."

The Kid — "Go ye and do likewise."

※　　　※　　　※

The minister had just been giving the class a lesson on the Prodigal Son. At the finish, to test what attention had been paid to his teaching, he asked, "Who was sorry that the Prodigal had returned?" The most forward youngster in the class breathlessly answered, "The fatted calf!" — *Home Herald*

※　　　※　　　※

Probably no man got so much conversation out of an operation as Adam did. — *Arkansas Gazette*

Teacher — "You remember the story of Daniel in the lion's den, Bobbie?"

Bobbie — "Yes, ma'am."

Teacher — "What lesson do we learn from it?"

Bobbie — "That we shouldn't eat everything we see."

— *Yonkers Statesman*

      ✳   ✳   ✳

"Johnny," said the teacher, "who were the two strongest men of olden times?"

"Samson and Hercules."

"Can you tell anything about them?"

"Oh, yes. Samson was a regular Hercules."

— *St. Louis Star*

      ✳   ✳   ✳

It isn't the style of the Bible that makes it unpopular with the moderns, but the fact that it crimps their style.

— *Pasadena Evening Post*

      ✳   ✳   ✳

In the window of a little bookstore on Eighth Avenue, N. Y., was recently heaped a great pile of Bibles marked very low — never before were Bibles offered at such a bargain; and above them all, in big letters, was the inscription:

"Satan trembles when he sees
Bibles sold as low as these."

— *Woman's Home Companion*

      ✳   ✳   ✳

"Will you tell me," the Sunday-school teacher was asked, "How far Dan is from Beersheba?"

Before the question could be answered, another party spoke up. "Do I understand Dan and Beersheba are names of places? I always thought they were husband and wife like Sodom and Gomorrah."

"There's Nebuchadnezzar eating grass like an ox," said one courtier. "Let's hope for the best," said the other. "Maybe he's trying to get even with the Babylonian beef trust."

— *Washington Star*

⚜   ⚜   ⚜

Teacher — "Can any little boy tell me how it was that David prevailed against the giant Goliath?"

Pupil — "My pa says brute strength never is in it with the feller with a pocketful of rocks." — *Boston Transcript*

⚜   ⚜   ⚜

A Frenchman is attempting to prove that Adam was a Frenchman. Judging from the swiftness of his fall, he might have been their first Premier. — *Punch*

⚜   ⚜   ⚜

"What system of fighting do you use?"
"Solomon's."
"What was that?"
"Well, he said a soft answer turneth away wrath."

⚜   ⚜   ⚜

A clergyman went to have his teeth fixed by a dentist. When the work was done the dentist declined to accept more than a nominal fee. The parson, in return for this favor, insisted later on the dentist accepting a volume of the reverend gentleman's own writing. It was a disquisition on the Psalms, and on the flyleaf he had to inscribe this appropriate inscription: "And my mouth shall show forth thy praise." — *Harper's Weekly*

⚜   ⚜   ⚜

Some day the Gideons who see to it that there's a Bible in each hotel guest room, are going to fix it so that the man who makes the hotel rates has one, too. — *Detroit Times*

One time Irvin S. Cobb was asked what one book he would rather have written than any other. His answer was:

"I would rather have written the Book of Job in the Old Testament than any other book in the world. I would rather have written it, because in it, I think, there is more of majesty, of poetry, of imagery, and of drama than in any work of similar length known to me."

※   ※   ※

W. S. Gilbert was lunching once at a country hotel, when he found himself in company with three cycling clergymen, by whom he was drawn into conversation. When they discovered who he was, one of the party asked Mr. Gilbert how he felt "in such grave and reverend company." "I feel," said Mr. Gilbert, "like a lion in a den of Daniels."   — *Boston Transcript*

※   ※   ※

The divine's keen wit was always based on sterling common sense. One day he remarked to one of his sons:

"Can you tell me the reason why the lions didn't eat Daniel?"

"No, sir. Why was it?"

"Because the most of him was backbone and the rest was grit."

※   ※   ※

It was visiting day at the insane asylum. One of the inmates imagined himself to be an artist, and he was busily engaged in dabbling at an empty canvas with a dry brush. A visitor, wishing to humor him, asked what the picture represented.

"That," said the patient, "is a picture of the Israelites being pursued through the Red Sea."

"Where is the sea?"

"Why, that's rolled back to allow the Israelites to pass."

"Where are the Israelites?"

"They've just gone by."

"Then where are their pursuers?"

"Oh, they'll be along in a minute."   — *Pup*

Baptism

The vicar was paying a visit to the houses of his poor parishioners. He asked the name of a youngster in one of the houses.

"Reginald d'Arcy Smif," replied the boy with a grin.

"Why did you give him a name like that?" turning to the father.

"Because I want him to be a boxer, and with a name like that he'll get plenty of practice at school."

    ✄   ✄   ✄

Minister (*at Baptism*) — "What is the name please?"

"Ralph Morgan Montgomery Alfred Van McGoof."

Minister (*to assistant*) — "More water please."

    ✄   ✄   ✄

"I'm going to call my baby Charles," said the author; "after Charles Lamb, you know. He is such a dear little lamb."

"Oh, I'd call him William Dean," said the friend. "He Howells so much."

— *Wisconsin Octopus*

    ✄   ✄   ✄

This notice is taken from a Kansas newspaper: "Positively no more baptizing in my pasture. Twice in the last two months my gate has been left open by Christian people, and I can't afford to chase cattle all over the country just to save a few sinners."

    ✄   ✄   ✄

Vicar (*filling Baptism record*) — "Let's see, this is the sixteenth, isn't it?"

"Lor' lumme, sir, no! Only the sixth."

Many ministers could, from personal experience, tell of strange names bestowed upon infants at their baptism, but few could equal the following story recently told by a bishop.

A mother who was on the lookout for a good name for her child, saw on the door of a building the word "Nosmo." It attracted her, and she decided that she would adopt it. Some time later, passing the same building, she saw the name "King" on another door. She thought the two would sound well together, and so the boy was baptized "Nosmo King Smith." On her way home from the church where the baptism had taken place, she passed the building again. The two doors on which she had seen the names were now closed together, and what she read was not "Nosmo King," but "No Smoking."

—The Argonaut

✕   ✕   ✕

Minister (*benevolently*) — "And what is your name my little man?"

Small Boy — "Well, if that isn't the limit! Why you baptized me!"

—Pittsburgh Gazette

✕   ✕   ✕

In a small church a child was to be christened. The young minister taking the little one in his arms said, "Beloved hearers, no one can foretell the future of this little child. He may grow up to be a great businessman like Henry Ford, or a great politician; and it is possible that he might become the prime minister of England. . . ."

Turning to the mother, he inquired: "What is the name of the child?"

"Mary Ann," was the reply.

—Wellington, N. Z., Newspaper

Bigotry

The famous actor, George M. Cohan had sent a telegram ahead to a town asking for reservations at a certain hotel. Came back the reply, "Sorry, we don't admit Jewish guests." Cohan wired back. "We were both wrong. You thought I was a Jew and I thought you were a gentleman."

✠　　✠　　✠

A young English girl went to a priest and said she wished to become a Catholic at once.

"But, my child, have you been properly instructed?" asked the priest.

"No, I have not, but that does not matter; I want to be made a Catholic now."

"But it does matter," argued the priest. "You must have several months instruction before you can possibly be received into the Church. May I ask what has made you think of taking this serious step?"

"Well," replied the girl, "I have had an awful row with my people, and I am determined to disgrace the family."

— *Southwest Courier*

✠　　✠　　✠

Bigotry has no head and cannot think, no heart and cannot feel. When she moves it is in wrath; when she pauses it is amid ruin. Her prayers are curses, her god is a demon, her communion is death, her vengeance is eternity, her decalogue is written in the blood of her victims, and if she stops for a moment in her infernal flight it is upon a kindred rock to whet her vulture fang for a more sanguinary desolation.

— *Daniel O'Connell*

One of the saints was brought before a magistrate who in anger told him he was going to tear his heart out.

The saint smiling, said, "It has been giving me a great deal of trouble of late."

⚐   ⚐   ⚐

The wit or wag who got away with the following bit of humor gives our idea of tolerance de luxe, *ne plus ultra, ad infinitum* and *e pluribus unum!*

Says the aforesaid wag — "My idea of tolerance is a baseball game between the Ku Klux and the Knights of Columbus, with a Negro umpire, and the proceeds of the game to go for the benefit of the Jewish Relief fund!"

— *Our City*

⚐   ⚐   ⚐

The man who preaches Prohibition in public and pays court to a gallon jug of corn juice in private; who damns the saloon at home and sits up all night with it abroad, may not transcend the law of the land, but if his Gall should burst the very buzzards would break their necks trying to get out of the country.

— *Wm. C. Brann*

⚐   ⚐   ⚐

A Kentuckian who fished more in the streams than he did in literature, was speaking one night before a number of fellow townsmen. After enthralling his listeners for a few minutes on the weird tales of the Catholic Church he ended up with this stirring appeal: "Yes sir, them Catholics is controlling everything. If we don't watch out they'll be erecting chasubles in our public squares."

Josh Billings

The following are some of the witty sayings of Josh Billings, America's famous humorist, on spiritual matters:

The devil owes most ov his success to the fackt that he iz alwuz on hand.

△ △ △

How menny people thare iz whoze souls lay in them, like the pith in a goose quill.

△ △ △

If I was asked which was the best way, in these days ov temp-tashum tew bring up a boy, i should say — bring him up the back way.

△ △ △

If i am charitable, if i am komplasent, if i am grateful, if i am honest, if i am virtewous — what ov it — i hav simply dun mi duty.

△ △ △

The most dangerous characters in the world are those who live in the subburbs of virtew.

△ △ △

There is no better evidence ov true friendship than tew speak of a man's vices tew hiz face, and ov hiz virtews behind hiz back.

△ △ △

Everyboddy in this world wants watching, but none more than ourselves.

△ △ △

Most people when they cum tew yu for advice cum tew have their own opinyons strengthened, not korrekted.

Choir

"What was that sentence the choir repeated so often during the litany?"

"As near as I could make out it was 'We are all miserable singers.'"

— *Boston Courier*

🐛   🐛   🐛

Dean Inge's favorite song should be "Lead Kindly Light." He seems to love the encircling gloom.

— *Philadelphia Inquirer*

🐛   🐛   🐛

"What are you children playing?" asked the mother.

"Church," chorused the crowd of youngsters.

"You know that you shouldn't whisper in church."

"Yes, but we're the choir."

🐛   🐛   🐛

A church choir is sometimes referred to as the War Department of the Congregation.

🐛   🐛   🐛

A Chicago reformer proposes the abolition of all church choirs. The movement for world peace continues to make rapid progress.

— *The Optimist* (Pittsburgh)

Church

Minister — "And what does your mother do for you when you are a good girl.".
"She lets me stay home from church."

✄ ✄ ✄

The building of a "skyscraper" church would seem to be a move in the right direction. — *Brooklyn Eagle*

✄ ✄ ✄

It was Smith's first Sunday as usher in church, and he was a bit flustered. Turning to a lady who entered he said: "This way, madam, and I'll sew you into a sheet." — *Boston Transcript*

✄ ✄ ✄

Pastor Bilk — "We must do something about the 'status quo.'"
"What is the 'status quo'?"
"That's Latin for 'the mess we're in.'"

✄ ✄ ✄

English Clergyman — "And when you arrive in London, my dear lady, don't fail to see St. Paul's and Westminster Abbey."
Fair American — "You bet, I'll rattle those off sure, but what I've been hankering to see ever since I was knee high to a grasshopper is the Church of England." — *Tid-Bits* (London)

✄ ✄ ✄

What is believed to be the longest name in the English language is the name of a town in Anglesea Wales. The name of this town is Llanfairpwelggwyngyllgogerychwyrndrobwellhandyssiliogogogoch. It has fifty-nine letters, in the postal directory only the first twenty letters are given. The name means, "The Church of St. Mary in a hollow of white hazel, near to the rapid whirlpool, and to St. Tisilio Church, near to a red cave."

✄   ✄   ✄

The Christian nations are those that have churches to stay away from on Sundays.

— Ex

✄   ✄   ✄

It's a question as to whether or not the churches are slipping but if they are it may be because they do not come out with a new model of religion every fall.

— Des Moines Register

✄   ✄   ✄

Pat and Isaac were good friends. One day Pat met Isaac coming out of the Catholic Church. "What are you doing here, Ike?" inquired Pat.

"Oh, the Father," said Isaac, "owes me a little bill and I'm taking it out in pew rent."

✄   ✄   ✄

The soldiers marched to the church and halted in the square outside. One wing of the edifice was undergoing repairs, so there was room for only about half the regiment.

"Sergeant," ordered the captain, "tell the men who don't want to go to church to fall out."

A large number quickly availed themselves of the privilege.

"Now, sergeant," said the captain, "dismiss all the men who did not fall out and march the others in — they need it most."

✄   ✄   ✄

The Rev. Harry Emerson Fosdick says that the modern church needs lubrication. Well, the Rockefellers belong to his church.

— New York American

THE SCIENTIST AND THE BUG

A scientist looked at a bug
  With his keen microscopical eye
And he said "What I see is a lesson to me
  That I'll never forget till I die.

For the infinitesimal bug
  Whether taken in part or in whole
From whisker and feeler to smeller and squealer
  Was under one central control.

Such unity built in a bug!"
  The scientist pondered and then
"If God will do that for a flea or a gnat
  Would He plan with less wisdom for men!

Would He fashion a Church for us here
  Through which all His blessings might flow —
With a unity less than this bug's — I confess
  That there's no other answer but, NO."

So the scientist led by the bug
  Started off on a diligent quest
For a unified church — and in all of his search,
  Only one measured up to the test.

And today people ask him, and smile
  When he answers their questioning shrug
And says in reply " 'Tis a fact sir, that I
  Was led into the Church by a bug."

— Arnott J. White in *To-Day's Parable*

✠　　　✠　　　✠

Some churches are so cold you could skate down the aisle.
— *Billy Sunday*

After a rousing plea for converts, a Methodist Negro preacher shouted, "Everybody come up and join de army of de Lord."

"I'se joined," replied one of the congregation.

"Whare'd yoh jine?" asked the exhorter.

"In de Baptis' ch'ch."

"Why, chile," exclaimed the minister, "yoh ain't in de army, yoh's in de navy."

          🙰   🙰   🙰

The church was crowded. The minister said he was very glad to see so many out to the Easter services, and as many of you will not be here again until next Easter, I want to take this occasion to wish you a Merry Christmas.

          🙰   🙰   🙰

"The building business seems to keep booming regardless," said Farmer Gray putting down the daily paper.

"Regardless of what?" asked his wife.

"Regardless of all the churches they're tearin' down. Yes sir—ee, we're tearin' down the churches, but we're buildin' bigger and better penitentiaries."

          🙰   🙰   🙰

A church at Haines City, Florida, says the *Washington Post,* is using rocking chairs instead of pews to seat the worshipers in comfort — newspaper filler — we don't believe churchgoers should be pampered any such way. If they can't sleep in pews, let 'em stay at home.

          🙰   🙰   🙰

The churches of the land are sprinkled all over with bald-headed sinners whose hair has been worn off by the friction of countless sermons that have been aimed at them and have glanced off and hit the man in the pew behind.

— Henry Ward Beecher

"A critic of our churches says they are dominated by a lot of old hens." Does he refer to the lay members?

— *Nashville Lumberman*

✄   ✄   ✄

First Verger — "Do you 'ave matins at your church?"
Second Verger — "No: we 'as linoleums."

— *The Sketch*

✄   ✄   ✄

There is an English church where a box hangs in the porch. It is used for communications for the pastor. Cranks put their notes in it, but occasionally it does fulfill its purpose. Recently the minister preached, by request, a sermon on "Recognition of Friends in Heaven," and during the week the following note was found in the box: "Dear Sir — I should be much obliged if you could make it convenient to preach to your congregation on 'The Recognition of Friends on Earth,' as I have been coming to your church for nearly six months, and nobody has taken any notice of me yet."

— *Christian Register*

✄   ✄   ✄

After the button factory closed in an Iowa town along the "Father of Waters," one of the local Fathers remarked, "No factory has contributed more to the churches of our country."

✄   ✄   ✄

"Going to church to show your new coat?"
"No, to show what a generous husband I got."

✄   ✄   ✄

Teacher — "Now, Robert, what is a niche in a church?"
Bobby — "Why, it's just the same as an itch anywhere else, only you can't scratch it as well."

— *Boston Transcript*

The Bishop of Muenster in Westphalen, Clemens August Count of Galen, preached in his Cathedral about the influence of the Church on the education of youth.

Suddenly a uniformed Nazi stood up and exclaimed — "How can anybody talk about youth if he himself has neither wife nor child?"

The Bishop answered in a thundering voice — "In this house I will allow no offensive remarks against the 'Fuehrer.'" (As is well known Hitler is not married.)

— *Brooklyn Tablet*

☒   ☒   ☒

"He was enclosed in a monastery of his absorbing interests."
— *Winifred Holtby*

☒   ☒   ☒

To say I don't need the Church is mere bravado. I needed it when my father died. I needed it when we were married, and when our babies were taken from us, and I shall need it again sooner or later and need it badly. I am in good health now, and I could, I suppose, get along nicely for a time without a clergyman or a choir or even a prayer. But what sort of a man is he who scorns and neglects and despises his best friend until his hour of tribulation?

— *Edgar A. Guest*

Clergymen

YOUR PARISH PRIEST

If you are trying to find the kind of a priest,
　Like the kind of a priest you like,
You needn't put your clothes in a grip
　And go on a long, long hike.

You'll only find what you left behind,
　For there is really nothing new
It's a knock at yourself when you knock the priest
　It isn't the priest — it's you.

You say he talks money each week,
　That's the only sermon we hear;
If every church member were just like you
　Would the church debt be clear?

The Parish is made by those not afraid
　Lest somebody else get ahead,
When a few do the work and the rest of you shirk
　No wonder the Parish is dead.

So support the church and your parish priest,
　Please remember this saying, too,
It's a knock at yourself when you knock the priest,
　It isn't your priest — it's you.

— Anon.

❈　　　❈　　　❈

"Yes," prattled the elderly lady, "that is the Duke and Duchess
and those on the right are the Vicar and — er — Vixen."

A minister was an accomplished naturalist and possessed a remarkable knowledge of different classes of fungi. One day while calling upon one of his parishioners who was ill, she reminded him of the long time that had elapsed since his last call. When he began to make excuses for the delay, she cut him short, "If I was a toadstool," she began with grim irony, "you'd have been to see me long ago."

      ✞   ✞   ✞

This one was told by Father Bernard Vaughn, who returned to his home in England after a long visit to this country. A visitor from South Africa, on being asked for his opinion of Niagara Falls, asked his American friend, in turn, "What do you think of Victoria Falls compared with Niagara?"

"Victoria Falls, compared with Niagara? — a mere frontal perspiration!"

— Brooklyn Eagle

      ✞   ✞   ✞

There once was a pious young priest,
Who lived almost wholly on yeast.
He said, "It is plain, we must all rise again,
So I want to get started at least."

— Selected

      ✞   ✞   ✞

Bishop Spalding of Louisville was the author of *The Life of Bishop Flaget* while Archbishop Kenrick of St. Louis wrote on *Anglican Orders*.

The two were at a gathering.

"Did you ever read my *Life of Bishop Flaget?*" asked the Louisville prelate.

"No, I never read any of those light works," said the archbishop.

"Well," said Bishop Spalding, "when I am suffering from insomnia, I read Kenrick's *On Anglican Orders.*"

A minister with two lovely girls, stood entranced by the beauties of a glowing stream. A fisherman happening by, and mistaking the minister's occupation, said: "Ketchin' many, pard?"

"I am a fisher of men," answered the preacher with dignity.

"Well," replied the fisherman, with an admiring glance at the girls, "you sure have the right bait."

— *Montreal Journal of Com.*

※   ※   ※

In Washington they tell the story of a golfing clergyman who had been beaten badly on the links by a parishioner thirty years his senior, and had returned to the clubhouse rather disgruntled.

"Cheer up," his opponent said. "Remember, you win at the finish. You'll probably be burying me some day."

"Even then," said the preacher, "it will be your hole."

※   ※   ※

A minister, spending a holiday in the north of Ireland, was out walking, and, feeling very thirsty, called at a farmhouse for a drink of milk. The farmer's wife gave him a large bowl of milk, and while he was quenching his thirst a number of pigs got round about him. The minister noticed that the pigs were very strange in their manner, so he said: "My good lady, why are the pigs so excited?"

The farmer's wife replied, "Sure, it's no wonder they are excited, sir; it's their own little bowl you are drinking out of!"

— *Tid-Bits*

※   ※   ※

A Texas paper comments: "The preacher has a great time. If his hair is gray, he is old. If he is a young man he hasn't had experience. If he has ten children he has too many. If he has none he isn't setting good example. If his wife sings in the choir, she is presuming; if she doesn't, she isn't interested in her husband's work. If a preacher reads from his notes he is a bore; if he speaks extemporaneously he isn't deep enough. If he stays at home in his study he doesn't mix with the people; if he is seen around the street he ought to be at home fixing up a good sermon. If he calls on some poor family he is playing to the grandstand; if he calls at the house of the wealthy, he's an aristocrat. Whatever he does someone could have told him to do better."

— The Churchman

※   ※   ※

The story is told that when Sidney Smith went to Brighton to reduce himself by certain baths in vogue at that time he met a friend who noticed the decrease in Smith's size and remarked of it to him.

"Yes," said Sidney, "I have been here only ten days and I have already taken off enough to make a curate."

※   ※   ※

A witty French abbé was once asked why he kept up a country seat which he never visited.

"Do you not know," he answered, "that I must have some place, where, though I never go to it, I can always imagine that I might be happier than where I am."

※   ※   ※

A well-known minister, famous for absentmindedness, once met an old friend in the street and stopped to talk with him. When about to separate, the minister's face suddenly assumed a puzzled expression. "Tom," he said, "when we met was I going up or down the street?"

"Down," replied Tom.

The minister's face cleared. "It's all right then. I had been home to lunch."

— New Outlook

※   ※   ※

A Protestant Episcopal minister was walking down a city

street wearing the garb of the profession. He was met by two Irish boys.

"Good morning, Father," said one of the boys.

"Hush, he ain't no father," said the other, "he's got a wife and two kids."

⋈   ⋈   ⋈

The only way a minister can meet his flock is to join a golf club.   — *American Golfer*

⋈   ⋈   ⋈

In a schoolboy's essay on clergymen, quoted by the *New Jersey Monitor*, divines are thus classified: "There are three kinds of clurgymen — bishups, vickers, and curits. The bishups tell the vickers to work and the curits do it. A curit is a thin married man; but when he is a vicker he gets fuller, and then he becomes a good man."

⋈   ⋈   ⋈

An old Indian from the Plains met a minister on Broadway. After speaking about conditions in the West the minister asked "Big Chief" what his business was. "Me preacher, too." "What is your salary?" asked the New York divine. "Two hundred dollars a year." "Tha's darn poor pay," replied the minister. "Well, me darn poor preacher," grunted the Indian.

⋈   ⋈   ⋈

A clergyman hearing of liberalism creeping into his parish said, "I hope it will soon strike the collection box."

⋈   ⋈   ⋈

A toast to the Papacy, so the story goes, was once proposed at a Hibernian banquet. Enthusiasm was running high and would not be restrained. More specific, more generous, more reckless grew the display of loyalty. "Not to the Papacy," they shouted, "we'll drink to all the Popes, one by one."

          — *The Historical Bulletin* (St. Louis Univ., St. Louis, Mo.)

Two parsons, after dining on a couple of chickens, were being conducted about the yard by the farmer host. A rooster was crowing on the fence with great gusto.

"My, he seems mighty proud of himself," said one of the clergy.

"He should," said the farmer, "he has two sons in the ministry."

※   ※   ※

A country boy feeling inclined to the ministry experienced a dream one night in which he saw two tall illuminated letters — P.C. — high in the sky. Arising the next morning, he took it as a vision, the letters being interpreted "Preach Christ."

Accordingly, he took his high-school, college, and seminary course. After his ordination, he found the ministry too difficult; results of his efforts practically nil. So meditating over the vision he concluded it didn't mean "Preach Christ," but rather "Plow Corn."

※   ※   ※

(Composed by a Sixth-Grade Lad in a Chicago Grammar School)

I want to be a priest. The reason I want to be a priest is because priests can't get married. All the priests live in a house next to the church. Priest's can't go to parties. And they stay home and go to bed early. No girls can bother them. That is why I would like to be a priest.

— *Line O'Type (Chicago Tribune)*

※   ※   ※

Cardinal Gibbons was traveling in the South. In New Orleans he was a guest at a gathering. Surrounded by the elite of beauty, the wealth and scholarship of the southern city, a stately lady, one who felt her own importance, was presented to the distinguished prelate. Greeting him she said, "I am so glad to meet Your Eminence as I have so much enjoyed your 'Decline and Fall of the Roman Empire.'"

The Archbishop of Canterbury was going in with a number of other clergymen to luncheon after some great ecclesiastical function, when an unctuous dignitary observed, "Now to put a bridle on our appetites!"

Quick as lightning the Archbishop retorted: "Say, rather, now to put a bit between your teeth."

— *Pathfinder*

✠   ✠   ✠

"You may say what you like against young ministers, but I have nothing but praise for our young pastor," the pompous Mr. Brown remarked, as he passed out of the church. "Nothing but praise!"

"So I observed," dryly retorted the deacon who had passed the plate.

— *Harper's*

✠   ✠   ✠

The Reverend Henry Ward Beecher
   Called a hen a most elegant creature.
The hen, pleased with that,
   Laid an egg in his hat,
And thus did the hen reward Beecher.

— *Oliver Wendell Holmes*

✠   ✠   ✠

Years ago I passed a group of boys playing on a vacant lot; I hailed them, "Hello, there, fellows." One little lad shouted back a kind of fresh, "Hello there, yourself, Mister."

Another boy corrected him in a stage whisper: "Shut up, Freddie: that is not a gentleman, he is a priest."

— Wynhoven, *Sacerdotal Salesmanship*

Collections

THE FABLE OF THE GOOD PEOPLE WHO RALLIED TO THE SUPPORT OF THE CHURCH

Geo. Ade

(With Special Permission)

A Congregation needed Money for repairing the Church, so the Women got together and decided to hold a Raspberry Festival. Sister Frisbie invited them to come and Carouse on her Front Lawn. Some 22 Members of the Flock flew out and bought a few Things to Wear, the Outlay for Washable Finery running to about $8 per Head.

Mr. Frisbie got $9 worth of Chinese Lanterns and strung them around. He wanted to do the Thing up Brown so as to get a Puff in the Weekly. The Paper came out and said that the Frisbie Front Yard with its Myriad Twinkling Lanterns was a Veritable Fairy-Land. That kind of a Notice is worth $9 of anybody's Money.

Mr. Frisbie and three other Pillars of the Church devoted $7 worth of Valuable Time to unloading Tables and Campstools.

The Women Folks ruined $14 worth of Complexion working in the Kitchen to make Angel Food and Fig Cake.

On the Night of the Raspberry Orgy the Public trampled down $45 worth of Shrubbery.

When it came time to check up the Linen and Silverware it was found that $17 worth of Spoons with Blue Thread tied around them had been lost in the Shuffle.

The Drip from the Candles ruined $29 worth of Summer Suits and Percale Shirt-Waists.

Four Children gorged themselves and each was tied in a True Lover's Knot with Cholera Morbus before another Sunrise. The Doctor Bills footed up $18.

After clearing the Wreck, paying the Drayman and settling for the Ice-Cream and Berries, it was discovered that the Church was $6.80 to the Good. So everybody said it was a Grand Success.
Moral: Anything to avoid dropping it in the basket.

※   ※   ※

LAMENT OF THE PEW

Locked one night in church, and asleep in a pew
Now did such a thing ever happen to you?
I'll never forget that Basilica so grand,
Renowned for its beauty all over our land
It was here that I heard near the midnight hour
A complaint from the pew. With increasing power,

The pew to the pulpit protested that night:
"Your Highness must know that it is my delight
To speak of your mission so high and sublime —
I've wanted to mention it many a time —
Our Lord has declared I should listen to you
For you are the pulpit and I, the pew.

"I'm hungry to hear of my Lord's Word today
I've waited a week — and at last it's Sunday
How much do I long for your message to men!
Your words are a comfort again and again.
But why do you speak at such length of collections,
And bingoes and dances are in your affections?

" 'Tis hungry I come and unfed go away
And still come again, hoping that on this day
I might hear you dwell on His loving Word —
But only the cries of the angels I heard
Lamenting with tears — for our Lord had said:
'My people are hungry! They MUST be fed!' "

— Harry J. Roche

CORRECT THIS SENTENCE — "I don't care, with the parish church and school and rectory that we have and with the services Father Smith gives us I wouldn't care if my pew rent were doubled."

※   ※   ※

A little girl had been taken to church for the first time. When she returned home her mother asked her what she thought of the church.

"I like it very much," she said, "but there was one thing I didn't think was fair."

"What was that, dear?"

"Why, one man did all the work and another man came around and got all the money."

※   ※   ※

Two church members met on the street on Monday morning. Said one, "I didn't see you in church yesterday."

"I know you didn't. I was taking up the collection."

※   ※   ※

Parishioner (*Sunday morning*) — "Give me change for a dime, please."

Storekeeper — "Sure, and I hope you enjoy the sermon."

※   ※   ※

Just before the collection was taken up one Sunday morning a Negro clergyman announced that he regretted to state that a certain brother had forgotten to lock the door of his chicken house the night before, and as a result in the morning he found that most of the fowls had disappeared. "I doan' want to be pussonal, bredr'n," he added, "but I hab my s'picions as to who stole dem chickens. I also hab reason fo' believin' dat if I am right in dose s'picions dat pusson won't put any money in de plate which will now be passed around." The result was a fine collection, not a single member of the congregation feigned sleep. After it was counted the old parson came forward. "Now, bredr'n," he said, "I doan' want your dinners spoilt by wonderin' where dat brudder lives who doan' lock his chickens up at night. Dat brudder doan' exist, mah friends. He was a parable gotten up fo' purpose of finances."

—The Tattler

✳   ✳   ✳

A mouse who lived in the pulpit for many years was disturbed by the preacher's pounding and shouting. One Sunday afternoon it sneaked out of its nesting place and strolling down the aisle met another mouse and told it about the disturbance.

"Come where I live," said the stray mouse, "and you won't be disturbed."

"Where is that?"

"In the poor box," replied the hermit mouse.

✳   ✳   ✳

A minister, in an address to other ministers, once said that he thought ministers ought to be humble and poor, like their Master. "I have often prayed," said he, "that I might be kept humble; I never prayed that I might be poor — I could trust my church for that."

—Ladies' Home Journal

✳   ✳   ✳

A minister consented to preach during his vacation in the country at an Episcopal church. When he arrived at the church on Sunday morning the sexton welcomed him and said: "Do you wish to wear a surplice, sir?"

"Brother," replied the minister, "I am a Methodist. What do I know about surplices? All I know is about deficits."

✳   ✳   ✳

The *London Catholic Times* printed the following letter which was sent by an Englishman to a well-known hospital in answer to an appeal for a donation:

"For the following reasons I am unable to send you a larger check: I have been held up, held down, sandbagged, walked upon, sat upon, flattened out and squeezed by the income tax, the Super Tax, the Tobacco Tax, the Beer Tax, the Spirits Tax, the Motor Tax, and by every Society, Organization and Club that the inventive mind of man can think of to extract what I may or may not have in my possession; for the Red Cross, the Black Cross, the Ivory Cross, the Double Cross and for every hospital in town and county. The Government has governed my business till I don't know who runs it. I am inspected, suspected, examined and re-examined, informed, required and commanded so that I don't know who I am, where I am, or why I am, or why I am here at all. I am supposed to be an inexhaustible supply of money for every need, desire or hope of the human race, and because I will not go out and beg, borrow or steal money to give away, I am cussed, discussed, boycotted, talked to, talked about, held up, hung up, rung up, robbed and well-nigh ruined. The only reason why I am clinging to life at all is to see what is going to happen next."

❈   ❈   ❈

Unnecessary — Pastor (*from the pulpit*) — "The collection which we took up today is for the savages of Africa. The trouser buttons which some of the brethren have dropped into the plate are consequently useless."

❈   ❈   ❈

A great many pennies had been put in the offering, and the vicar's attention was called to this. One night he held up a silver dollar and a copper penny, and gave a conversation held by the two coins. "You poor little red cent; you don't amount to anything. I'd hate to be you," said the big dollar. "I know I'm not very big," replied the cent, "but the children like me, and I can buy a good many things." "Huh! you can't buy anything at all," said the dollar. "Just look at me, big and bright and shiny. I can buy a whole lot more than you can." "Maybe so," said the little red cent, meekly, "but I go to church a heap oftener than you do."

✄   ✄   ✄

"My sermon on thrift made a tremendous impression on the congregation."
"How do you know?"
"I could tell when I counted the collection."

— *Home Sector*

✄   ✄   ✄

"Penny wise and pound foolish," soliloquized the man in church and he put the penny in the box and the pound into his pocket.

✄   ✄   ✄

Will members of the congregation who wish to put buttons in the collection use their own and stop tearing them off the hassocks.

— *London Tattler*

✄   ✄   ✄

One day, not long since, a parishioner of our State was out hunting. During the day a rainstorm came on. In order to keep dry he crawled into a hollow log. When the rain began to fall the log began to swell, until he could get neither way. He thought his end had come. He thought of all the wrongs he had done, and when he recalled that he had not paid his church dues for several years he crawled out of the log through a knothole.

✄   ✄   ✄

"Won't you give a shilling to the Lord?" said a Salvation Army girl to an old Aberdonian.
"How auld are ye, lassie?" he inquired.

"Nineteen, sir."

"Ah, weel, I'm past seventy-five. I'll be seein' Him afore you, so I'll hand it to Him mysel'."

—*Times of India*

✄   ✄   ✄

"When I look at this congregation," said a preacher, "I ask myself, 'Where are the poor?' And then when I look at the collection I say to myself, 'Where are the rich?'"

✄   ✄   ✄

COMPENSATION*

Elsie Janis

When my luck seems all out
And I'm down at the mouth,
When I'm stuck in the North,
And I want to go South;
When the world seems a blank
And there's no one I love,
And it seems even God's
Not in Heaven above,
I've a cure for my grouch
And it works like a shot —
I just think of the things that
   I'm glad I am not:
A bird in a cage,
A fish in a bowl,
A pig in a pen,
A fox in a hole,
A bear in a pit,
A wolf in a trap,
A fowl on a spit,

---

* With special permission of the author and the copyright owners. Copyright by Cosmopolitan Co.

A rug on a lap,
A horse in a stable,
A cow in a shed,
A plate on a table,
The sheet on a bed,
The case on a pillow,
A bell on a door,
A branch on a willow,
A mat on the floor.
When I think of the hundreds of
    things I might be,
I get down on my knees and
    thank God that I'm me.
Then my blues disappear, when I
    think what I've got,
And quite soon I've forgotten the
    things I have not.

✘   ✘   ✘

A Quaker once hearing a person tell how much he felt for another who was in distress and needed assistance, dryly asked him, "Friend, has thee felt in thy pocket for him?"

—*The Christian Evangelist*

✘   ✘   ✘

"Five pounds! Is that all the squire is giving to the church fund? Why he ought to give fifty," exclaimed the squire's wife.

"Ah," said the vicar in a soft voice, "I suspect he forgot the 'ought.'"

✘   ✘   ✘

The father wanted to test the generous nature of his son, so as the boy was going to church one morning he said:

"Here, Benny, are a quarter and a penny. You can put whichever you please in the contribution box."

Benny thanked his papa and went to church.

Curious to know which coin Benny had given, his papa asked him when he returned, and Benny replied:

"Well, papa, it was this way. The preacher said the Lord loved a cheerful giver, and I knew I could give a penny a good deal more cheerfully than I could give a quarter, so I put the penny in."

— Ladies' Home Journal

✄   ✄   ✄

A minister had a son born to him and was given a generous donation from his church the other Saturday, and in the next day's prayer he alluded with gratitude to the arrival of a little succor.

✄   ✄   ✄

There was a wise man who said, "Odd
If the Heavenly path could be trod
By spending your cash
Upon pleasures and trash,
And not spending any on God."

Death

One day a fairy came to a man and told him she would grant him any favor he might wish. The man thought a few minutes, and then said, "My wish is to see a newspaper published one year from today." Immediately the fairy handed him the newspaper printed one year in advance. He turned quickly to the financial page, ran his finger nervously up and down the list of stocks, and leaping from his chair shouted, "Hurrah! I'm worth fifteen million dollars. Isn't that wonderful?" Then carelessly turning over to the obituary page his glance fell on a report that made him gasp. "Great Heavens! I died two days ago."

✠　　　✠　　　✠

An eastern bishop who had prepared several times for death recalled the story of the Scotchman, who, condemned to be hanged by his chief and availing himself of the privilege of his clan, which allowed him to select the tree on which he was to be suspended, selected a bush not three feet high, answered when taunted with his stupidity: "I am in no hurry — I can wait till it grows."

✠　　　✠　　　✠

Parson — "Poor Mrs. Anderson. It is a hard blow for you to be made a widow, but still there is a comforter for you."
Widow — "What is his address?"

— Lawyer and Banker

✠　　　✠　　　✠

Rector (*going his rounds*) — "Fine pig that, Mr. Dibbles; uncommonly fine!"
Contemplative Villager — "Ah, yes, sir; if we was only all of us as fit to die as him, sir!"

— Tid-Bits

A rich man who was on his deathbed, called his chauffeur who had been in his service many years, and said,

"Ah, Sykes, I'm going on a long rugged journey, worse than ever you drove me."

"Well, sir," consoled the chauffeur, "there's one comfort, it's all down hill."

— American Legion Weekly

          ❧   ❧   ❧

I'll sing you a song of the world and its ways
   And the many strange people we meet,
From the rich man who rolls in his millions of wealth
   To the struggling wretch on the street.

But a man though he's poor and in tatters and rags,
   We should never affect to despise,
But think of the adage, "remember, my friends,
   That six feet of earth, make us all of one size."

          ❧   ❧   ❧

A story comes from Vienna, where it is reported that 1,500 Jews had committed suicide after Hitler took possession of the country.

This joke actually aims to squeeze a laugh out of suicide, which any professional humorist will tell you is a pretty hard job.

The story has it that Levi on meeting Cohen says:

"It's terrible. Moritz has gone and committed suicide." To which Cohen replies:

"Well, why shouldn't a man take a chance to better his position, if he can."

          ❧   ❧   ❧

His Master's Voice — "What were your father's last words?"

"There were no last words. Mother was with him to the end."

— Outlaw

I am in my eighty-second year, and my number is up, and my cremation furnace may make an end of me any moment, to the great relief of many worthy persons.

— *George Bernard Shaw*

✖   ✖   ✖

Quizly — "Do automobiles stop for funerals?"
Father Alfred — "Stop for them? Man alive! they make them."

✖   ✖   ✖

When Benjamin Franklin was asked whether or not he would like to live life over again, he replied, "Yes, provided, of course, that you allow me the author's privilege of correcting the second edition."

✖   ✖   ✖

I hate funerals and would not attend my own if it could be avoided, but it is well for every man to stop once in a while to think what sort of a collection of mourners he is training for his final event.

— Robert T. Morris, *Fifty Years A Surgeon*

✖   ✖   ✖

A lot of sinners are playin' the game of life like Notre Dame's football team — waitin' for the last minute to win the game. These sinners, you'd think, were wanting to give their heavenly spectators an eleventh-hour thrill. The Old Nick is pushin' them all over the field, spittin' in their eye, spikin' their shins, throwin' them for losses and penalizing 'em back to Sodom and Gomorrah. As Bill Nye used to say, you can lose your health and regain it, you can lose your wealth and regain that too, but if you lose your soul "It's good-by, John."

— *Source Unknown*

Devil

There were several passengers. One believed himself to possess a fund of humor which he intended to expend on a priest who got in at one of the intermediate stations. Bestowing a patronizing look on the clergyman, he said:

"Have you heard the news, Monsieur le curé?"

"No, my friend, I have not," was the reply. "I have been out all day, and have not had time to glance at the papers."

Then said the traveler: "It is something dreadful; the devil is dead."

"Indeed," replied the ecclesiastic, without the smallest surprise or displeasure. Then, seeming deeply touched, he added: "Monsieur, I have always taken the greatest interest in orphans. Will you accept these two sous?"

✻   ✻   ✻

"Satan is represented as runnin' after folks wif a pitchfork," said Uncle Even, "which de truth is dat so many folks is pullin' at his coat tails dat he ain't got time to chase nobody."

— *Washington Star*

✻   ✻   ✻

"If the devil himself came to New York, I verily believe that some preachers could be found to serve on the reception committee. They call that sort of thing 'liberality and breadth of view.' I call it supine and cowardly connivance with iniquity."

— *Rev. J. R. Straton*

✻   ✻   ✻

Of course, Satan has some kind of a case, it goes without saying. It may be a poor one, but that is nothing; that can be said about any one of us. — We may not pay him reverence for that

42

would be indiscreet; but we can at least respect his talents. A person who has for untold centuries maintained the imposing position of spiritual head of four fifths of the human race, and political head of the whole of it, must be granted the possession of executive abilities of the loftiest order. — I would like to see him. I would rather see him and shake him by the tail than any other member of the European Concert.

— *Mark Twain*

#

There was formerly a tavern in Fleet Street, near Temple Bar, known by the sign of the Devil and St. Dunstan. It was much frequented by lawyers as a place for dining and was noted for the excellence of its liquors. It was familiarly called the Devil. When a lawyer from the Temple went to dinner there, he usually put a notice on his door, "Gone to the Devil."

Some who had neglected business, frequently had this notice exhibited, until at length "Gone to the Devil" became synonymous with gone or going to ruin.

#

"What became of the evil spirits that were cast into the swine?"

"They made them into deviled ham."

— *Steele's Lion* (Dayton)

#

The difference between spirit doctors and doctored spirits is that the latter really show you the next world.

— *Washington Post*

#

A teacher asked her Sunday-school class what was meant by a man "possessed of evil spirits."

"A bootlegger," one youngster spoke up.

An old Irishman who had recently recovered from a severe attack of sickness, chanced to meet his parish priest, who had been summoned during his illness to administer the rites of the church to the dying, as he was considered to be near death's door, and the following conversation took place: "Ah, Pat, I see your out again. We thought you were gone sure. You had a pretty serious time of it."

"Yis, yer riverence, indade I did."

"When you were so near death's door were you not afraid to meet your God, your Maker?"

"No, indade, your riverence. It was the other gintlemin."

✖　　　　✖　　　　✖

First Devil — "Ha, Ha! Ho, Ho!"

Satan — "Why all the mirth?"

First Devil — "I just put a woman into a room with a thousand hats and no mirror."

— *The Coal-Getter*

✖　　　　✖　　　　✖

"There's the devil to pay at my house!"

"Better to go to church then."

"Well, there's the preacher to pay."

— *Atlanta Constitution*

✖　　　　✖　　　　✖

Satan, according to one Western clergyman, is busy in the colleges.

In that respect Satan differs from the great mass of undergrads.

— *New York Times*

✖　　　　✖　　　　✖

Two Irishmen were gazing at the wonderful dome of St. Peter's in Rome.

"Sure, Mike," said Pat, "it beats the devil."

"Faith, and that was the intention," replied Mike.

A teacher in one of the Chicago schools called an incorrigible to her desk, and grasping his arm firmly, said:

"Young man! The devil certainly has hold of you!"

"Guess yer right, mum."

— *The Bohemian*

✠   ✠   ✠

"If the devil lost his tail, where would he go?"

"To a liquor store where they retail spirits."

✠   ✠   ✠

The preacher spoke of the joys to come and the reverse. "You all got your choice," he said. "Will you take the good side or the bad? Will you have wings or not?" After the sermon a smart young sport accosted him. "Parson," he said, "ah done got a problem in ma head." "What's yo' problem, Brother?" rumbled the parson. "Dis yer's de problem, Parson. How am ah goin' to get ma coat on over ma wings?" "Dat ain't yo' problem, Brother," said the parson with scorn. "Yo' problem's goin' to be — how'll yo' get yo' hat over yo' horns?"

✠   ✠   ✠

Now the Faith is old, and the Devil is bold —
    Exceedingly bold indeed;
And the masses of doubt that are floating about
    Would smother a mortal creed.

But we who sit in a sturdy youth
    And still can drink strong ale —
Let us put it away to infallible Truth
    That always shall prevail.

— *Hilaire Belloc*

Drink

"What means this W.C.T.U.
  Which makes such constant fuss?"
The maiden frowned, "I thought you knew
  That Whiskey Can't Touch Us."
                        — *New York Tribune*

⚜   ⚜   ⚜

A bishop was in the car that knocked down a drunken man. The bishop fearing the man was killed alighted in a great state of anxiety. The man, however, was little hurt and when he saw the bishop he let forth a torrent of profanity.

"My friend," said the bishop, "never in my life have I heard such language, but never in my life have I been so pleased to hear any language at all."

⚜   ⚜   ⚜

A priest was addressing his congregation on the dangers of intemperance.

"Drink, my friends, makes you beat your wives, starve your families, shoot your landlords — yes, and miss them, too."

⚜   ⚜   ⚜

Curate — "You should be careful! Don't you know that drink is man's worst enemy?"

Jeems — "Yes; but don't you teach us to love our enemies?"
                        — *London Opinion*

⚜   ⚜   ⚜

The minister met Tom, the village ne'er-do-well, and much to the latter's surprise, shook him heartily by the hand.

"I'm glad you turned over a new leaf, Tom."

46

"Me?" asked Tom dubiously.

"Yes, I saw you at church last evening."

"Oh, is that where I was?"

During a minister's clerical convention, one of the ministers had an experience he will long remember. He was a portly man, weighing over three hundred pounds. While walking through Boston Common he sat down on one of the benches to rest. When he attempted to get up, he failed in the effort. He tried again and failed. About this time a little girl, poorly clad, came along and was attracted by the struggles. Stepping up to him, she exclaimed:

"Don't you want me to give you a lift?"

The minister gazed at her in amazement and exclaimed, "Why, you can't help me. You are too little."

"No, I am not," she replied. "I have helped pa get up many times when he was drunker than you are."

— *Homiletic Review*

During the flu epidemic in San Francisco, when all public meeting places were closed, and the entire population was compelled to wear masks to prevent the disease, a drunken man was overheard muttering: "Well, I'm an old man, but I have lived my time and am ready to quit. I have lived to see four great things come to pass — the end of the war, the churches closed, saloons left open, and the women muzzled."

— *Judge*

Colonel Bob Maxe, it is said, is responsible for the following witty toast to water:

"Ladies and gentlemen," began the colonel, "you have asked me to respond to the toast 'Water,' the purest and best of all the things that God has created. I want to say to you that I have seen it glisten in the tiny teardrops on the sleeping lids of infancy; I have seen it trickle down the blushing cheeks of youth, and go in rushing torrents down the wrinkled cheeks of age. I have seen it in tiny dewdrops on the blades of grass like polished diamonds, when the morning sun burst in resplendent glory over the Eastern hills. I have seen it in the rushing river, rippling over pebbly bottoms; roaring over precipitous falls, in its mad rush to join the Father of Waters. And I have seen it in the mighty oceans on whose broad bosoms float the battleships of the world, but, ladies and gentlemen, I want to say to you now, that as a beverage, it is a failure."

❈   ❈   ❈

Two men who were slightly intoxicated were unsteadily standing in front of a liquor-store window. One started to laugh uproariously.

"Now look at that bottle there," said one, "it says, 'Vat 69.' You know I always thought that was the Pope's telephone number."

❈   ❈   ❈

One would hardly expect from the pen of the scholarly Canon Liddon an excursion in light verse. The following lines, however, in *Jack O'London's Weekly,* are said to have been written by the Canon when he had been bored by the speech of a teetotal lecturer:

> Pure water is the choicest gift
>   That man to man can bring.
> But who am I that I should want
>   The best of everything?
>
> Let princess revel with the tap
>   Kings with the pump make free;
> Whisky, wine or even beer
>   Is good enough for me.

— *Ave Maria*

Drives

The local church was making a drive for funds, and two colored sisters were bearing down hard on Uncle Rastus.

"I can't give nothing!" exclaimed the old Negro. "I owe nearly everybody in this here old town already."

"But," asked the collectors, "don't you think you owes de Lawd somethin' too?"

"I does, sister, indeed," said the old man, "but He ain't pushin' me like my other creditors is."

※　　　※　　　※

A country pastor who evidently has troubles of his own, is having heart-to-heart talks with his delinquent parishioners. The following is one of the latest:

"Good morning. Have you paid your church dues this year? Perhaps you owe for last year, or several years. Now, you understand we don't need money; we have millions — to get. But it is really an imposition to let people go on carrying our money when we are strong and healthy and so abundantly able to bear the burden ourselves. For this reason we ask anybody who has any of our money in his possession to leave it at the rectory or send it by post, freight train, express, or any other way, just so it gets here. Silver and gold are heavy, and it would be a matter of lifelong regret if anybody should get bowlegged carrying it about for us."

※　　　※　　　※

In his announcement on a Sunday morning, the vicar regretted that money was not coming in fast enough — but he was no pessimist.

"We have tried," he said, "to raise the necessary money in the usual manner. We have tried honestly. Now we are going to see what a bazaar can do."

— *Savannah News*

※   ※   ※

A minister in a certain town in Alabama took permanent leave of his congregation. His farewell talk:

"Brothers and Sisters, I come to say good-by. I don't think God loves this church because none of you ever die. I don't think you love each other, you never marry each other. I don't think you love me because you don't pay my salary. Brethren, I am going to a better place. I have been called to be a chaplain in a penitentiary. I go to prepare a place for you and may the Lord have mercy on your souls."

— *Fashion Magazine*

※   ※   ※

A parson wrote to his bishop asking him to come and hold a "quiet day." The bishop declined, saying, "Your parish does not need a quiet day; it needs an earthquake."

— *Christian Register*

※   ※   ※

"Was the charity ball a success?"

"Oh, yes, indeed. They say the gowns must have cost a half million at least."

"And how much was raised for charity?"

"Why, nearly $700. Wasn't that fine?"

— *Cleveland Plain Dealer*

※   ※   ※

Little Milton came home from Sunday school with a mite box. "Why do they call it a mite box, mother?" asked Milton.

"Because," said his brother, "you might put something in it and you might not."

— *The Churchman*

Mark Twain used to tell the story to illustrate the value of the brevity of speech. Twain began by saying that he went to church one Sunday morning, and the preacher began a passionate appeal to save the heathen. The humorist listened for five minutes and was willing to give fifty dollars. After ten minutes more of listening he reduced the amount to twenty-five. After another half hour he reduced it to five, finally when the plate was passed Twain took two dollars out of the collection.

❈ ❈ ❈

An old Southern planter met one of his former Negroes whom he had not seen for a long time. "Well, well!" said the planter, "what are you doing now, Uncle Amos?"

"I'se preaching of de gospel."

"What! you preaching?"

"Yassah, marster, I'se a-preachin'."

"Well, well! Do you use notes?"

"Nossuh. At de fust I use notes, but now I demans de cash."

— *New Success*

❈ ❈ ❈

In a certain home-missionary movement every participant was to contribute a dollar that she had earned herself by hard work. The night of the collection of the dollars came, and various and droll were the stories of earning the money. One woman had shampooed hair, another had made doughnuts, another had secured subscriptions, and so on.

The chairman turned to a handsome woman in the front row. "Now, madam, it is your turn," he said. "How did you earn your dollar?"

"I got it from my husband," she answered.

"Oh!" said he. "From your husband? There was no hard work about that."

The woman smiled faintly. "You don't know my husband," she said.

— *Ladies' Home Journal*

A Philadelphia minister started a campaign against lipstick — as if the young men of the country hadn't been setting their faces against it for years.

✄   ✄   ✄

Mabel — "Was your bazaar a success?"

Gladys — "Yes, indeed; the minister will have cause to be grateful."

Mabel — "How much were the profits?"

Gladys — "Nothing. The expenses were more than the receipts. But ten of us got engaged, and the minister is in for a good thing in wedding fees."

— Stray Stories

✄   ✄   ✄

The method by which our wives in America are knocking the church debt silly, by working up their husbands' groceries into "angel food" and selling them below actual cost, is deserving of the attention of our national financiers. The church debt itself is deserving of notice in this country. It certainly thrives better under a republican form of government than any other feature of our boasted civilization.

— Bill Nye

Epitaphs

St. Albans boasts a man who revels in the patronymic of Stonegraves. That name is tomb much for us. Well, it is cemeterial whether you like it or not.

※ ※ ※

Billie — "Pa?"
Father — "Well, son?"
Billie — "Pa, I took a walk to the cemetery today and I read inscriptions on the tombstones."
Father — "What did you think about the writing on them?"
Billie — "Well, I was just wondering where all the bad people were buried."

※ ※ ※

"When I die," Will Rogers once said, "my epitaph, or whatever you call those signs on gravestones, is going to read:

" 'I joked about every prominent man of my time, but I never met a man I didn't like.'

"I am proud of that. I can hardly wait to die, so it can be carved, and when you come around to my grave you'll probably find me sitting there proudly reading it."

— *New York Herald Tribune*

※ ※ ※

A committee on collections approached an Irish grocer with a request for a donation to build a fence around the cemetery. He refused.

"What's the use of buildin' a fince," said he, "them that's in can't get out an' them that's out don't want to get in."

— Whalen, *Byways of Humor*

53

The tombstone of a certain genial host bears his name and 'his inscription, "This Is On Me."

   ✄   ✄   ✄

"I suppose," said a sympathizing neighbor, "that you will erect a handsome monument to your husband's memory." Then says the *New York Press,* the tearful widow replied: "To his memory! Why John hadn't any. I was looking through his clothes today and I found his pockets full of letters that I had given him to post."

   ✄   ✄   ✄

In Webley churchyard, York, there is this inscription:

> This tombstone is a Milestone;
> Ha! how so?
> Because beneath lies MILES who's
> Miles below.

An epitaph in Bath Abbey:

> Here Lies Ann Mann
> She lived an old maid
> And she died an old Mann.

And gloomy Sullen's epitaph runs thus:

> Here lies John Sullen, and it is God's will
> He that was Sullen should be sullen still.
> He still is sullen, if the truth ye seek:
> Knock until doomsday. Sullen will not speak.

Away back in an Italian cemetery is this lovely wording on a tomb:

> Here lies Estella
> Who transported a large fortune to heaven
> In acts of charity,
> And has gone thither to enjoy it.

In a cemetery at Middlebury, Vermont, is a stone, erected by a widow to her loving husband bearing this inscription:
"Rest in peace — until we meet again."

— The Jewish Ledger

        ✄   ✄   ✄

Here lies Mary, the wife of John Ford,
We hope her soul is gone to the Lord,
But if for Hell she has chang'd this life
She had better be there than be John Ford's wife.

        ✄   ✄   ✄

The Body
of
Benjamin Franklin
Like The Cover Of An Old Book,
Its Contents Torn Out
And Stript Of Its Lettering And
Gilding (Lies Here Food For Worms);
Yet The Work Itself Shall Not Be Lost
For It Will (As He Believed) Appear
In A New
And More Beautiful Edition
Corrected and Amended
By
THE AUTHOR

        ✄   ✄   ✄

Sooner shall these mountains crumble
Into dust than shall Argentines and
Chileans break the covenant which at
The feet of Christ, the Redeemer,
They have sworn to maintain.

The above inscription is found on the bronze figure of Christ, twenty-six feet high on the line separating Chile and Argentina.

A farmer wandering around a cemetery, came upon a stone which bore the inscription, *"Sic transit gloria mundi."*

"What does that mean?" he asked the sexton.

The sexton not wishing to confess ignorance, replied, "Well, it means he was sick transiently and went to glory Monday."

✕ ✕ ✕

"To follow you
  I'm not content
'Til I find out
  Which way you went!"

✕ ✕ ✕

How now who is heare?
I, Robin of Doncastere
That I spent, that I had;
  That I gave, that I have;
That I left, that I lost.

✕ ✕ ✕

In Ohio, they tell of a young widow who, in consulting a tombstone-maker with reference to a monument for the deceased, ended the discussion with:

"Now, Mr. Jones, all I want to say is, 'To My Husband' in an appropriate place."

"Very well, ma'am," said the stonecutter.

When the tombstone was put up the widow discovered, to her amazement, that upon it were inscribed these words:

To My Husband.
In An Appropriate Place

— *Harper's*

✕ ✕ ✕

A certain man left his wife money to pay for a stone to his memory. She carried out the letter of the bequest by buying a diamond.   — *Pathfinder*

God

A little girl was put in an upper berth of a Pullman sleeping car for the first time. She kept crying until her mother told her not to be afraid, because God would watch over her. "Mother, you there?" she cried. "Yes." "Father, you there?" "Yes." A fellow passenger lost all patience at this point and shouted: "We're all here! Your father and mother and brothers and sisters and aunts and uncles and cousins. All here; now go to sleep." There was a pause; then, very softly: "Mamma!" "Well?" "Was that God?"
— *Tid-Bits*

✤ ✤ ✤

An instructor in a church school where much attention was paid to sacred history, dwelt particularly on the phrase "And Enoch was not, for God took him." So many times was this repeated in connection with the death of Enoch that he thought even the dullest pupil would answer correctly when asked in examination: State in the exact language of the Bible what is said of Enoch's death.

But this was the answer he got: "Enoch was not what God took him for."
— *Brooklyn Life*

✤ ✤ ✤

At one of the public receptions in the White House, an old gentleman from Buffalo, as he shook hands with "Honest Abe," remarked,

"Up our way we believe in God and Abraham Lincoln."

To this the President characteristically replied:

"My friend, you are more than half right."

✤ ✤ ✤

"Eternity is the lifetime of God."
— *Anon.*

57

Colonel Lawrence of Arabian fame tells how an Arab sheik, after hearing what a Western astronomer revealed that he had seen in the telescope said, "You foreigners see millions of stars, and nothing beyond. We Arabs see only a few stars and God."

✝ ✝ ✝

"What sort of luck did Father McCoy have hunting moose up in Canada?"

"Oh, Father shot wonderfully well, but Providence was very merciful to the moose."

✝ ✝ ✝

Pastor — "So, God has sent you two more little brothers."

Dolly (*brightly*) — "Yes, and He knows where the money's coming from. I heard daddy say so."

✝ ✝ ✝

In the cathedral of Lubeck in Germany there is the following inscription found on a slab:

"Ye call Me Master, and obey Me not;
Ye call Me Light, and see Me not;
Ye call Me Way, and walk Me not;
Ye call Me Life, and desire Me not;
Ye call Me Wise, and follow Me not;
Ye call Me Fair, and love Me not;
Ye call Me Rich, and ask Me not;
Ye call Me Eternal, and seek Me not;
Ye call Me Gracious, and trust Me not;
Ye call Me Noble, and serve Me not;
Ye call Me Mighty, and honor Me not;
Ye call Me Just, and Fear Me not;
IF I CONDEMN YOU, BLAME ME NOT.

✝ ✝ ✝

Don Seitz, in his life of Joseph Pulitzer, tells a story of a young reporter on the *New York World* who was sent to cover a revival meeting, and to whom, in the midst of the proceedings, an exhorter bent and said: "Will you not come forward?"

"Excuse me," was the reply, "but I am a reporter and am here only on business."

"But," said the revivalist, "there is no business so momentous as the Lord's."

"Maybe not," said the reporter, "but you don't know Mr. Pulitzer."

※　　　※　　　※

"Stonewall" Jackson had the following to say in regard to keeping God always in his mind: "When I take my meals there is the grace. When I take a draught of water I always pause, as my palate receives the refreshment, to lift up my heart to God in thanks and prayer for the water of life. Whenever I drop a letter in the box, I send a petition along with it for God's blessing upon its mission and upon the person to whom it is sent. When I break the seal of a letter just received I stop to pray to God that He may prepare me for its contents and make it a messenger of good."

※　　　※　　　※

A man was told who had been complaining about his misfortunes, "You should be trusting in Providence and satisfied with your lot."

"A lot?" he exclaimed, "I'd be satisfied with a little."

※　　　※　　　※

A little colored boy who had been drilled to be respectful in speaking of his elders was asked in catechism how many persons there are in God.

"Three: the Fathah," he began slowly, "the Son," and after a pause of head scratching, "Ah's forget the otheh gen'leman's name."

A letter addressed "To God in Heaven, up in the sky" was found in the Minneapolis post office. The letter was opened and it was found that it was written by a little six-year-old boy to his best pal, a little four-year-old chum, recently deceased. The contents of the letter read, "Dear God, When I go upstairs please let me see Floydie." Bobby. This letter got national publicity in the secular papers of the U. S. The boy's name — Bobby Lewis.

✘   ✘   ✘

The keeper of the seals for Louis XIII one day asked a little boy, "Where is God? Tell me that and I'll give you an orange."

"You tell me where He isn't and I'll give you two oranges," replied the little fellow.

✘   ✘   ✘

A young man was trying to impress upon his Sunday-school class the infinite power of the Creator.

"Did you ever stop to think of the marvelous power of the All-Wise Father? The same power that lifted the everlasting hills, fashioned the babbling rill; the same power that creates the cyclone, sends the fragrant zephyr; the same power that made me, made a daisy."

✘   ✘   ✘

The farmer was complaining to the minister of the terrible bad weather for crops when the minister reminded him that he had much to be thankful for. "Providence cares for all. Even the birds of the air are fed each day."

"Yes," said the farmer, "off my corn."

✘   ✘   ✘

A little six-year-old, whose parents were of the Calvinistic faith, was very much surprised on hearing that Jesus was a Jew. "I don't see how that could be," she retorted, "when God, His Father, was a Presbyterian."   — *Lippincott's Magazine*

It will be recalled when the Saviour was brought before Pilate, the Roman governor asked Him, "What is truth?" In the Latin text of the Vulgate the question runs, *"Quid est veritas?"* The answer is found in the question itself, without adding or taking away a single letter. By rearranging the letters we get the answer, *"Est vir qui adest,"* which translated gives us, "It is the man who stands before you."

𝖷   𝖷   𝖷

It was noon at the mosque. The high priest was intoning, "There is but one God and Mohammed is His prophet."

A shrill voice broke in, "He is not."

The congregation turned around as one, and among the sea of brown faces could be distinguished one small yellow face.

The genial priest straightened up and smiled, "There seems to be a little Confucian here," he said.

𝖷   𝖷   𝖷

When the new puppies were discovered to be blind Teddy was very unhappy. His auntie assured him that God would open their eyes in due time. When bedtime came Teddy was heard adding a petition to his prayers. "Dear God, do please hurry up and finish those puppies!"   — *Lippincott's Magazine*

𝖷   𝖷   𝖷

Said the teacher to Willie: "Why, Willie, what are you drawing?"

"I'm drawing a picture of God."

"But, Willie, you mustn't do that; nobody knows how God looks."

"Well," he said, "they will when I get this done."

𝖷   𝖷   𝖷

Of course Americans trust in God. You can tell that by the way they drive.   — *Sharon Herald* (Pa.)

Hymn

A worthy missionary in India had the hymn "Rock Of Ages" translated into Hindustani. On retranslation into English by a student, the first two lines bore this inspiring and illuminating aspect:

"Very old stone, split for my benefit,
Let me absent myself under your fragments."

— *The New York Times*

✄　　　✄　　　✄

A well-known bishop relates that while on a recent visit to the South he was in a small country town, where, owing to the scarcity of good servants, most of the ladies preferred to do their own work.

He was awakened quite early by the tones of a soprano voice singing, "Nearer, My God, To Thee." As the bishop lay in bed he meditated upon the piety which his hostess must possess which enabled her to go about her task early in the morning singing such a noble hymn.

At breakfast he spoke to her about it, and told her how pleased he was.

"Oh, law," she replied, "that's the hymn I boil the eggs by; three verses for soft and five for hard."

— *St. Jos. News Press*

✄　　　✄　　　✄

"What three things does a bride think of during the wedding march?"

"Aisle, altar, hymn."

The Sunday-school teacher said, "Now we'll try that hymn again — 'Little drops of water' — and put some spirit into it."

             ✄   ✄   ✄

The Sunday-school teacher asked the children to write down the name of their favorite hymn.

One little girl wrote down, "Willie Smith."

Heaven

THE BISHOP'S STORY

A hot debate was on one night at the Rapparees Club. Long Austhy contended that it was easy to get into Heaven. Michael Flynn stoutly argued that Purgatory, the in-between place, called for a long stay. McCormack placidly expressed the hope he would be lucky enough to get to Purgatory.

"For thin," said he, "no matter how long I stay, I'm sure of Heaven."

Tim Feeney thought there were different degrees of detention, and that bishops, by reason of their great responsibilities, were there a long while.

Michael Flynn, with a sly smile said, "If ye all hould yeer whist, I'll prove ye are wrong."

When he had our attention, he proceeded as follows:

"A Sister of Charity died and went up to the Golden Gates. She knocked on the door, and it opened, and a voice asked:

" 'Who is it?'

" 'Sister Mary Aloysius, good St. Peter,' said the dear soul.

" 'What is your record, Sister?'

" 'Well, good St. Peter, I entered religion at the age of sixteen, and all my life was spent in caring for the poor, and on the battlefields, and in the hospitals.'

" 'A very good record indeed, but not enough to admit you to Paradise. Please stand aside.'

"The poor Sister was bewildered, but she meekly moved over beyond the Gate. Then up came an Irishman and knocked loud on the gate.

" 'Who is it?' said the voice.

" 'Who is it? Haven't ye me name here?'

"The voice replied, 'You are not here to ask questions but to answer. What is your name?'

" 'Patrick John Maguire, yer honor.'

" 'And from whence do you come, Patrick John Maguire?'

" 'Philadelphia, yer Honor.'

" 'And what is your record?'

" 'What's me record?' says Maguire, 'Haven't ye it all written down?'

" 'You were told not to ask questions,' said the voice, 'but to answer.'

" 'Oh,' says Maguire, 'I have a fine record. Worked hard all me life, never missed Mass, raised a family of nine children, an' three of them entered religion. How's that for a record?'

" 'A very good record indeed,' said St. Peter, 'but not enough to let you enter. Please stand aside.'

" 'Wait a minute,' said Pat, 'send for St. Patrick.'

" 'No,' said St. Peter, 'we do not allow any pull at the Gate.' Patrick moved over beside the Sister.

" 'Hard luck, Sister,' says he.

" 'Indeed, Patrick,' said the Sister, 'I do not understand it.'

"While they were talkin' up came a very imposin' dignitary, and thundered on the Gate.

" 'Who is it?' asked the voice.

" 'The Lord Bishop of Granada.'

" 'Come right in your Lordship.'

" 'Did you see that, Sister?' asked Pat.

" 'Alas! I did, Patrick, but still I do not understand.'

"Pat looked down the road, and says he, 'Wait a minute, Sister, I have a schame that will get us both in.'

"So down the road he went, and came back with a large bag, which he laid at the feet of the Sister.

" 'Now, Sister,' says he, 'if you will just step into that bag, I will put you over my shoulder, and we will both get in.'

"Well, the poor Sister thought she might as well try it, so she did so. Pat very respectfully drew the top of the bag up over her head, put her over his shoulder, and advanced to the Gate. This time he kicked the Gate.

" 'Who is it?' said the voice.

" 'The Lord Bishop of Granada's luggage,' roared Pat.

" 'Come right in.' "

— Whalen, *Byways of Humor*

🦋   🦋   🦋

The late Wilbur Wright put safety above everything else in airplane construction. Mr. Wright was once watching with a critical eye the flight of a very swift, very cranky airplane, when a little girl said to him: "Uncle Wilbur, can you get to heaven in one of those machines?" "Not by going up," replied the great airman, "but if you have lived a very good life you may do so by coming down."

🦋   🦋   🦋

When Barnum toured Europe with his circus, he went to pay his final respects to the Bishop of London before sailing.

"I hope I see you in heaven," said the venerable cleric.

"You'll see me if you're there," said Barnum.

🦋   🦋   🦋

Sunday-School Teacher — "If you are a good boy, Willie, you will go to heaven and have a gold crown on your head."

Willie — "Not for mine, then. I had one of them things put on a tooth once."

— *Puck*

🦋   🦋   🦋

It was after closing time in Heaven and there was a loud and even peremptory bang on the door. "Who's there?" asked Peter. "It is I," said a voice outside. "I say, Paul," said the janitor, "get all those teachers to move up! 'It's me,' has always been the correct use of the French idiom, '*C'est moi*.' "

— John O'Connor in *The Tablet* (London)

"What a fine place Heaven must be," said a little boy.

"Why do you think so, sonny?"

"Because the nails of the floor up there are so grand."

✖   ✖   ✖

They were homeward bound from church. "According to the minister's sermon this morning," said Mrs. Enpeck, "there is going to be no marrying or giving in marriage in heaven. Do you believe that?"

"Well, I have no reason to doubt it," answered Enpeck. "There must be some way to distinguish it from the other place."

✖   ✖   ✖

In a small village in Ireland the mother of a soldier met the village priest, who asked her if she had had bad news. "Sure I have," she said. "Pat has been killed."

"Oh, I am very sorry," said the priest. "Did you receive word from the War Office?"

"No," she said, "I received word from himself."

The priest looked perplexed, and asked, "But how is that?"

"Sure," she said, "here is the letter; read it for yourself."

The letter said, "Dear Mother — I am now in the Holy Land."

— *The Argonaut*

✖   ✖   ✖

It seemed that when Rastus and Sam died they took different routes, so when the latter got to heaven he called Rastus on the phone.

"Rastus," he asked, "how you like it down thar?"

"Oh, boy! Dis here is some place," replied Rastus. "All we have to do is to wear a red suit wid horns, an' ebery now an' den shovel some coal on de fire. We don't work no more dan two hours out ob de twenty-four down here. But, tell me, Sam, how is it with you up yonder?"

"Mah goodness! We has to get up at fo' o'clock in de mawnin' an gathah in de stars; den we has to haul in de moon and hang out de sun. Den we has ter roll de clouds aroun' all day long."

"But, Sam, how comes it yo' has ter work so hard?"

"Well, to tell de truf, Rastus, we's kin' o' short o' help up here."

— *Philadelphia Public Ledger*

    ✄   ✄   ✄

George, who lives in London, happened to meet the vicar of his native parish the other day, and eagerly asked after some of his old acquaintances.

"And old Mr. Jones?" he asked. "Have you seen him?"

The vicar shook his head. "I shall never see him again," he answered slowly, "Mr. Jones has gone to heaven."

— *Tid-Bits*

    ✄   ✄   ✄

"O, I wish I had the wings of a grasshopper," exclaimed a colored woman at a revival meeting.

"Amen," exclaimed several voices.

After the meeting the old lady was asked why she had made that remark.

"That I might fly to heaven," she replied.

"You fool nigger, a woodpecker would ketch you before you got half way there."

    ✄   ✄   ✄

Up there the sheep and goats will be divided, but down here the sheep are usually the goats.

— *Eugene Daily Guard*

    ✄   ✄   ✄

Joan — "Mummy, was baby sent down from heaven?"

Mother — "Yes, dear."

Joan — "They do like to have it quiet up there, don't they?"

— *The Passing Show* (London)

St. Peter — "Awfully good of you to come! Walk right in and I'll introduce you to the company."

Bashful Young Man — "Are you quite s — sure that this is h — heaven?"

— Life

※ ※ ※

A very wealthy man went up to Heaven and St. Peter was showing him around the place. The wealthy man was surprised to find that his servants all had mansions to live in, similar to the kind he had on earth. In great hopes, he asked St. Peter to show him his home in the skies. Pointing over to the slum section of the place, St. Peter showed him a poor, tumbled-down, unpainted shack, with the shingles coming off, and the broken windows stuffed with newspapers.

"What," cried the gentleman in surprise, "you mean to say that this is my home in Heaven, and my servants live in such splendid palaces?"

"Right," answered St. Peter. "You see, the homes in Heaven are built from the materials you send up here while you are on earth. That's the kind of stuff you sent up, you see."

※ ※ ※

A little girl asked her mother if there were any men in heaven.

"Mamma," she said, "I never saw a picture of an angel with a beard or mustache. Do men ever go to heaven?"

"Oh, yes," replied the mother, "but it's always by a close shave."

※ ※ ※

An Italian bishop who had borne many trials tells how he attained mastery over himself. "By making the right use of my eyes," said he, "I first look up to Heaven as the place where I am going to live forever. I then look down upon earth and consider how small a space of it I can soon occupy or want. I then look around me and see how many are far more wretched than I am."

John D. Rockefeller took a little girl in Cleveland to ride in his car and, after she had comfortably seated herself, he asked her, "Where would you like to go?"

"Oh, I don't care," the little miss replied. "Where do you want to go?"

"I," Mr. Rockefeller replied with a twinkle in his eyes, "I want to go to heaven."

"Oh, Mr. Rockefeller," the girl exclaimed, "I guess you haven't got gasoline enough to take you there."

— *Boston Globe*

    ✄   ✄   ✄

A preacher in Tennessee once speaking of heaven said, "My brethren, there will be a great many surprises for you if you reach the kingdom of heaven: you will look around you expecting to find a lot of people who won't be there: you will see many people there who you did not expect to get in; but the last and greatest surprise will be that you got in yourselves."

    ✄   ✄   ✄

A man once said to Bishop Wilberforce, "Pray, sir, can you tell a plain man in a single sentence the way to go to Heaven?"

"Certainly," said the Bishop. "Turn to the right and go straight ahead."

    ✄   ✄   ✄

Little Betty was explaining to her little brother how wrong it is to work on Sunday.

"Why," said the boy, "policemen work on Sunday. Don't they go to heaven?"

"No," explained the little girl, "they are not needed there."

    ✄   ✄   ✄

"If the wrong side of heaven is beautiful," said a little girl, looking at the stars, "what must the right side be?"

"God doesn't run excursions to Heaven. You must pay the full fare. Your religion is worth just what it costs you. If you get religion and then lie down and go to sleep, your joints will get as stiff as old Rip Van Winkle's did, and you will never win a religious marathon. . . . Some preachers I know of have study cushions that need half soling more than their shoes do. But I can say the same about all of you — add a 100 per cent to it, double that, and still not be in gunshot of the truth. Some people work only with their mouth. God wants your hands and feet as well. He wants YOU — ALL of you."

— Wm. A. Sunday

A Sunday-school teacher was quizzing her class of boys on the strength of their desire for righteousness.

"All those who wish to go to heaven," she said, "please stand."

All got to their feet but one small boy.

"Why, Johnny," exclaimed the shocked teacher, "do you mean to say that you don't want to go to heaven?"

"No, ma'am," replied Johnny promptly. "Not if that bunch is going."

— Delineator

St. Peter — "Here is your golden harp."

Newly Arrived American — "How much is the first installment?"

Another good thing about treasures in Heaven is that they cannot be reached by an inheritance tax.

— N. Y. Evening Journal

St. Peter — "How did you get here?"

New Arrival — "Flu."

He turned around, gazed at his wife in the back seat, and said, "Aw, shut up. I know what I am doing. An' doncher forgit it." One minute later St. Peter was handing him a flute with six holes and told him to move over in the alto section.

— *Florida Times Union*

                  ✳   ✳   ✳

Apropos the floods in the east is Donald F. McPherson's story about a hero of the Johnstown flood of '89 who died and went to heaven. Asked his identity by St. Peter, he expatiated at some length on his activities during the flood, relating how many lives he had saved, both human and animal. A little group gathered inside the gate of heaven and listened respectfully, with the exception of a little old man with a long white beard. He made contemptuous sounds throughout the narrative and when the Johnstown-flood hero had concluded his tale, the little old man gave a long raz-z-z-berry.

"Don't mind him," said St. Peter, observing the Pennsylvanian's startled look. "That's only Noah."

— June Provines in *Chicago Tribune*

Hell

During revival meetings in a Western city placards giving notices of the various meetings, subjects, etc., were posted in conspicuous places. One day the following was displayed:

Subject — "Hell: Its Location and Its Absolute Certainty."

"Thomas Jones, baritone, will sing, 'Tell Mother I'll Be There!'"
— *Ladies' Home Journal*

❦ ❦ ❦

One of the bravest, as well as one of the wittiest things that has been done lately, was the reply of an eastern minister when the representative of one of the worst of modern newspapers asked him for "a bright, terse interview about hell" for its Sunday edition. Doctor Smyth very kindly complied with the request. His article was as follows: "Hell, in my opinion, is the place where the Sunday edition of your paper should be published and circulated."
— *News-Letter*

❦ ❦ ❦

Small Boy — "Mamma says you are a very rich man."

The Visitor — "Your mother exaggerates, Willie; I'm not so very rich."

Small Boy — "Ain't you rich enough to go to hell?"
— *Life*

❦ ❦ ❦

A spiritualist had a message from her husband to send him a package of cigarettes.

"Where shall I send them," she asked a friend, "he didn't give any address."

"Well," said the friend, "you notice he didn't ask for matches. That's a kind of an indication."

A colored preacher down South was trying to explain the fury of hell to his congregation.

"You all is seen molten iron runnin' out from a furnace, ain't you?" he asked.

The congregation said it had.

"Well," continued the preacher, "dey uses dat stuff for ice cream in de place what I'm talkin' 'bout."

☒   ☒   ☒

The favorite expression of a kindly old Irishman, no matter what the event or calamity befell, was, "It might be worse." One day a friend said to him, "I have something to tell you, and you won't be able to use your favorite phrase. I dreamt last night that I died and went to hell." "It might be worse," said the old man. "Man alive, how could it be worse?" "It might be true," said his friend.   — Whalen, *Byways of Humor*

☒   ☒   ☒

Two women were discussing the first sermon of the young curate.

"An' how did it go?" inquired one.

" 'Twas the finest I ever heard. 'Twas all about hell," answered the other.

"Sure," said the first one, "I have known him since he was an innocent bit of a boy, an' what would a pious lad like him know about hell?"

"Well," said the second woman, "if you heard the sermon, an' all he knew about it, ye'd have said he was born and raised there."

☒   ☒   ☒

The story is told of a bishop traveling in the West. A boisterous cowboy got on the train and sitting down by the prelate inquired, "Where in 'ell did I see you before?"

"What part are you from?" rejoined the bishop.

The spiritualist was communicating with her deceased husband.

She — "Are you happy where you are, dear?"

He — "Oh, my, yes."

She — "Are you happier than when you were here with me."

He — "Yes, indeed I am."

She — "Heaven must be wonderful."

He — "Probably it is, but I'm not there."

    ✄   ✄   ✄

"The new House chaplain does not believe in hell."

"Give him time. He'll get over that before Congress adjourns."

— *Toledo Blade*

    ✄   ✄   ✄

Billy Sunday's sermons sound to us like Dante's "Inferno" translated by a baseball reporter.

— *Chicago Daily News*

    ✄   ✄   ✄

"Don't know what Hades is
But have a large-sized hunch
That there at every meal
You're served a picnic lunch."

Ku Klux Klan

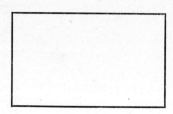

Picture of a Ku Klux Klan meeting held on an Indiana snow-field (never mind how many!), years ago.

❊ ❊ ❊

Still the klan that wears evening gowns is more dangerous than the one that wears nightgowns.

— *New Britain Herald*

❊ ❊ ❊

China favors the Klan, with an eye to the laundry work.

— *Wall Street Journal*

❊ ❊ ❊

We wish to thank neighbors and friends, and especially the members of the K. K. K., who so kindly assisted in the death and burial of our father and uncle.

— *Card of Thanks*

❊ ❊ ❊

"Frank's initials are K.K.K. aren't they?"
"Yes."
"How's that?"
"Well, you see the minister who baptized him stuttered."

The Klan is against World Court. It would be against heaven for the same reason — neither is 100 per cent American.

— Norfolk Virginia Pilot

🗶 🗶 🗶

No wonder the Ku Klux Klan is asleep with all their night shirts and bunk.

🗶 🗶 🗶

Cannibalism has disappeared from the American continent, but the Democrats still roast a Negro occasionally.

— St. Joe Herald

🗶 🗶 🗶

In the days when Al Smith was touring the country seeking the presidency and the white-robed Klan were burning fiery crosses and denouncing Catholics, Jews, and Negroes, there were two friends, a priest and a minister in an Alabama town who never let the crusade of bigotry mar their friendship.

During his evening services the minister had a box in which questions on religious topics were submitted for him to answer from the pulpit. Naturally, many sly digs were made at his associating with the Papist. One evening, taking up the slip of paper on which was a question, his face glowed with satisfaction as he looked benignly at his congregation.

"Now here," says the minister, "is a question that the priest in town could answer better than I can, but I think I can give one answer to it at least. The question is, 'Why does a priest wear his collar backwards like a horse?' Now there may be better answers than the one I'm going to give, but I'd say the reason a priest wears his collar backwards is to distinguish him from the jackass that asked this question."

Lying

Two Methodist preachers, one white and the other colored, served rural charges in Mississippi which were coterminous. The Negro received a considerably larger salary than his white brother, who asked him if it was not his custom to expel his members who failed to pay. "No, boss," he replied, "we would not like to put the gospel on a money basis. We gets them to subscribe, and if they don't pay we turns them out for lying."

— *Memphis Commercial*

❈　　❈　　❈

The vicar was addressing the school on the subject of truth. He expounded at some length on the wickedness of lying, and before going on to the merits of speaking the truth he thought he would see if the children really understood him.

"Now," said he, "can anyone tell me what a lie is?"

Immediately a number of small hands shot up. The vicar selected a bright-looking youngster.

"Well, my little man?"

"Please, sir, a lie is an abomination unto everyone, but a very pleasant help in time of trouble."

— *Lutheran Observer*

❈　　❈　　❈

A minister who was walking along a road saw a crowd of boys surrounding a dog.

"What are you doing with the dog?" asked the kindly minister.

"Whoever tells the biggest lie, he wins the dog."

"Oh, my, my, my," exclaimed the minister, "when I was a little boy like you here I never told a lie."

There was a moment's silence. "Here," said one of the little fellows, "you win the dog."

An evangelist conducting services announced that next Sunday he would speak on liars. He advised them for the better understanding of his lecture, to read in preparation the seventeenth chapter of St. Mark.

When Sunday came, he ascended the pulpit, and asked: "I would like to know how many of you read the seventeenth chapter of St. Mark, as I advised last Sunday?"

A hundred or more hands went up.

"Now," said the preacher, "you are the very ones to whom I wish to talk. There is no seventeenth chapter in St. Mark."

— Kremer, *Electrons of Inspiration*

❈   ❈   ❈

Little Nelly told little Anita what she termed a "little fib."

Anita — "A fib is the same as a story, and a story is the same as a lie."

Nelly — "No, it's not."

Anita — "Yes, it is, because my father said so, and my father is a professor at the university."

Nelly — "I don't care if he is. My father is a real estate man and he knows more about lying than your father."

— *The Delineator*

❈   ❈   ❈

"Behind the altar," said the cathedral guide to a party of tourists, "lies Richard II. In the churchyard outside lies Mary Queen of Scots. And who" — halting above an unmarked flagging in the stone floor and addressing a tourist from London — "who do you think, sir, is a-lying 'ere on this spot?"

"Well," answered the Cockney, "I don't know for sure, but I have my suspicions."

— *Tid-Bits*

❈   ❈   ❈

Once a fisherman, always a liar.

— *Old Proverb*

Here is a pretty quibble from the edition of "Logic for the Million," which Sharper Knowlson prepared:

> David said in his wrath, All men are liars.
> Therefore, David was a liar.
> Therefore, what David said was not true.
> Therefore, David was not a liar.

But if David was not a liar, what he said was true; namely, that all men are liars.

— New York Globe

❊   ❊   ❊

Mary — "Do liars go to heaven, mother?"
Mother — "Of course not, darling."
Mary — "My! Mother, George Washington must be lonesome up there."

❊   ❊   ❊

A little child was asked why God doesn't strike everybody dead when they tell a lie, just like he did Ananias and Sapphira.

"Because," said the little fellow, "there wouldn't be anybody left."

❊   ❊   ❊

Before Bishop Wade returned from the United States to his remote diocese in the Solomon Islands, he told of a cross questioning to which one of his black chiefs was submitted, "Do you like the bishop?" "We like the bishop." "Do you like the government?" "We no like the government." "Why don't you like the government?" "Government white man." "But the bishop is a white man." "Bishop no white man; bishop say true." In the eyes of the primitive black "white man" means "deceiver."

— Catholic World

Marriage

Archbishop Ryan was visiting a small parish in a mining district one day for the purpose of administering confirmation, and asked one nervous little girl what matrimony is.

"It is a state of terrible torment which those who enter are compelled to undergo for a time to prepare them for a brighter and better world," she said.

"No, no," remonstrated her rector, "that isn't matrimony: that's the definition of purgatory."

"Leave her alone," said the Archbishop, "maybe she is right. What do you and I know about it?"

— Ladies' Home Journal

❧   ❧   ❧

As the vine, which has long twined its graceful foliage about the oak, and been lifted by it into sunshine, will, when the hardy plant has been rifted by the thunderbolt, cling round it with its caressing tendrils, and bind up its shattered boughs; so it is beautifully ordained by Providence, that woman, who is the mere dependent and ornament of man, in his happier hours, should be his stay and solace when smitten with sudden calamity; winding herself into the rugged recesses of his nature, tenderly supporting the drooping head, and binding up the broken heart.

— Washington Irving

❧   ❧   ❧

At a public dinner a speaker spoke for half an hour and looked like going on for another thirty minutes.

A guest turned to a woman next to him and remarked: "Can nothing be done to shut this man up?"

"Well," responded the other cheerfully and frankly, "I've tried for fifteen years."

— Vart Hem.

A justice of the peace in Oklahoma, was called upon to perform the marriage ceremony for a young couple.

The Judge, who until a short time before had gained his legal knowledge in a neighboring state, where ministers officially officiate on such occasions, was at a loss to know how to proceed. However, he arose to the occasion. Commanding the couple to stand up, he directed that they be sworn in the following terms:

"Do you solemnly swear that you will obey the Constitution of the United States and The Constitution of the State of Oklahoma, and perform the duties of your office to the best of your ability, so help you God?"

The couple nodded assent. Then, continued the judge. "By the power in me vested by the strong arm of the law I pronounce you man and wife, now, henceforth, and forever, and you will stand committed until the fines and costs are paid, and may the Lord have mercy on your souls."

— *Philadelphia Ledger*

※   ※   ※

A little girl in church watching a wedding, suddenly exclaimed, "Mamma, has the lady changed her mind?"

"What do you mean?" the mother asked.

"Why," replied the child, "she went up the aisle with one man and came back with another."

※   ※   ※

"If marriage makes two persons one, it's obvious," said Morrell, "the maxim's wrong that says, 'It takes two to make a quarrel.'"

— *Selected*

※   ※   ※

A pastor who had discussed marriage was criticized by a middle-aged woman who said, "You can't appreciate the difficulties of marriage, Father. You never were married yourself."

"No, I wasn't," said the priest, "and I never laid an egg, but I am a better judge of an omelet than any hen in the state."

A recent experience of a Virginia clergyman throws light on the old English law requiring that marriages should be celebrated before noon. A colored couple appeared before him, asking to be married, the man in a considerably muddled state. The minister said to the woman, "I won't perform this ceremony."

"Why is dat, boss?" she queried. "Ain't de licenses all right? An' we is of age."

"Yes, but the man is drunk. Take him away and come back again." Several days later the couple again presented themselves the man once more obviously intoxicated. "See here, I told you I wouldn't marry you when this man was drunk," the minister said testily. "Don't you come back here till he's sober."

"Well, you see, suh," the woman replied apologetically, "de trufe is dat he won't come less'n he's lit up."

— *The Argonaut* (San Francisco)

※　　　※　　　※

He met her in Friendship, Missouri, followed her to Love, Virginia, and asked her to name the day at Ring, Arkansas. They were married at Church, Iowa, settled down at Home, Oregon. Twins were born at Boise, Idaho, and christened at Waterbury, Connecticut.

※　　　※　　　※

At a revival meeting the evangelist, working himself up to the height of emotionalism, after having spoken upon the weakness of mankind in general, suddenly exclaimed:

"Who is the perfect man? Is there such a being? If anyone has ever seen the perfect man let him say so now."

A small, nervous man rose quietly in the rear of the hall. The evangelist gazed at him in astonishment.

"Do you mean to say sir, that you know who is the perfect man?"

"I certainly do."

"Who may he be?"

There was a breathless silence as the man paused before answering, "My wife's first husband."

❈   ❈   ❈

An Irishman was taken to court for failure to support his wife. The case was a plain one against the man. The judge asked the wife, "Have you any other means of support?" "Yes, Your Honor, I have to tell the truth. I have three."

"What are they?" asked the judge.

"Me two hands, Yer Honor, me good health, and me God."

❈   ❈   ❈

"Ole," said the preacher to the Swedish bridegroom-to-be, "do you take Hilda Sorgeson for your lawful wedded wife, for better or for worse?"

"Oh, well," replied Ole gloomily, "Aye s'pose Aye get little of each."

— *The American Legion Weekly*

❈   ❈   ❈

The Gay Divorcee Guide (*to actress*) — "There's a lot of people outside to see you. Among them is a bishop who says he married you some time ago."

"Gee, I'm practically certain I never married a bishop."

❈   ❈   ❈

"Louise, I really cannot permit you to read novels on Sunday."

"But, grandma, this novel is all right; it tells about a girl who was engaged to three clergymen, all at once."

— *Life*

❈   ❈   ❈

"How many of the movie stars can you name that weren't in a divorce court?"

"Well there was 'Rin-Tin-Tin,' the canine actor."

"Susannah," asked the preacher, when it came her turn to answer the usual question in such cases, "do you take this man to be your wedded husband, for better or for worse — "

"Jes' as he is, pahson," she interrupted, "Jes' as he is. Ef he gits any bettah Ah'll know de good Lawd's gwine to take 'im; an' ef he gets any wusser, w'y Ah'll tend to 'im myself."

— *Youth's Companion*

     ✖   ✖   ✖

Mrs. Reed (*with newspaper*) — "It says here that a woman in Omaha has just cremated her third husband."

Her daughter commented, "Isn't that just the way. Some of us can't get one and some of us have husbands to burn."

     ✖   ✖   ✖

The minister advertised for a man servant and next morning a nicely dressed man rang the bell.

"Can you start the fire and get breakfast by seven o'clock?" inquired the minister.

"I guess so."

"Well, can you wash the dishes, polish the silver, and keep the house nice and tidy?"

"Say parson, I came here to see about getting married, but if it's all that, count me out."

     ✖   ✖   ✖

The pastor had preached a good sermon on marriage. Two old Bridgets waddled slowly out at the close of the service. "Ah, 'twas a fine sermon his rivirence was after a'givin'."

"Indade it was," said her friend, "an' I wish I knew as little about it as he does."

     ✖   ✖   ✖

Many delicate compliments have been paid the fair sex by men subtle in speech, but the following comes straight from the heart of an illiterate Negro, who was married in the South by a white minister. At the conclusion of the marriage the groom asked the price of the service.

"Oh, well," answered the minister, "you can pay me whatever you think it is worth to you."

The Negro turned silently, looked his bride over from head to foot; then, slowly rolling up the whites of his eyes, said:

"Lawd, sah, you has done ruined me for life; you has, for sure."   — *Harper's Monthly*

✄   ✄   ✄

Deacon — "By the way, that man Brown you married a year ago, has he paid you for your fee yet?"

Clergyman — "No; the last time I reminded him of it he said I'd be fortunate if he didn't sue me for damages."

— *Boston Transcript*

✄   ✄   ✄

"Statistics prove that marriage is a preventive against suicide," said Mrs. Gabb.

"Yes," growled Mr. Gabb, "and statistics also prove that suicide is a preventive against marriage."   — *Cincinnati Enquirer*

✄   ✄   ✄

A gentleman formerly attached to the American Embassy at London tells how an old country sexton in a certain English town, in showing visitors around the churchyard, used to stop at one tombstone and say:

"This 'ere is the tomb of 'Enry 'Ooper an' 'is eleven Woives."

"Eleven!" exclaimed a tourist on one occasion. "Dear me! That's rather a lot, isn't it?"

Whereupon the sexton, looking gravely at his questioner, replied:

"Well, mum, yer see, it war an 'obby of 'is'n."

— *Harper's*

Mr. McDonald (*arranging with clergyman for his second marriage*) — "And I should like the ceremony in my yard this time, sir."

Clergyman — "Good gracious, why?"

Mr. McDonald — "Then the fowls can pick up the rice — we wasted a deal last time!"

— *London Opinion*

⚜   ⚜   ⚜

SOCIETY ITEM

Miss Jennie Jones and Bog Henry were married at the Jones' mansion last evening. The bride is a daughter of Constable Jones, who has made a good officer, and will undoubtedly be re-elected this spring. He offers a fine horse for sale in another column of this paper. The groom runs a store on Main Street and is a steady customer of our advertising columns. They were married by Rev. Josiah Butterworth, who called at this office last week and gave us a nice order for handbills. Jennie and Bog left on the one o'clock train for Chicago to visit the bride's uncle, who we understand, has lots of money and a cancer.

— *Watseka (Ill.) Republican*

⚜   ⚜   ⚜

Friends often asked Marie Corelli why she never married. "There is no need," she would reply, "for I have three pets at home which answer the same purpose as a husband. I have a dog which growls all morning, a parrot which swears all the afternoon, and a cat which comes home late at night."

Missionaries

"Their prepublication office (of *Time*) was a room in a two-story frame house on Manhattan's East 18th Street. Between their desks stood a large iron kettle — about the size and shape used by African cannibals for the boiling of missionaries."

— *Time Magazine*

Missionary — "I hear your chief is an author."
Native — "Yes, he has just finished a digest of European missionary."

Several years ago a little girl, Helene McKenna, wrote the following interesting and humorous letter to the *Far East,* a missionary magazine:

"I want a Chinese baby," she said. "Send me one with a pigtail. I'd like one with red hair. Mamma says I can have one to play with, so I am sending ten cents and a stamp. I don't want a baby that's always crying; for I just hate crybabies, and mamma does too. I am six years old. I have red hair and blue eyes, and I'm Irish."

In darkest Africa, two natives were watching a leopard chasing a missionary.
"Can you spot the winner?" asked one of the spectators.
"The winner is spotted," replied the other.

A missionary probably has a hard time making savages believe that they should wear modern clothes.

— *Trinidad Picketwire*

A man soliciting aid for foreign missions, was refused with the reply: "I don't believe in foreign missions. I want what I give to benefit my neighbors."

"Well," rejoined the caller, "whom do you regard as your neighbors?"

"Why, those around me."

"Do you mean those whose land adjoins yours?"

"Yes."

"How much land do you hold?"

"About five hundred acres."

"And how far through the earth do you own?"

"Why, I have never thought of it before, but I suppose I own it half way down."

"Exactly. I suppose you do, and I want this money for the heathen whose land adjoins yours at the bottom."

❌   ❌   ❌

Missionary (*explaining to visitors*) — "Our situation was so remote that for a whole year my wife never saw a white face but my own."

Sympathetic Young Woman — "Oh, the poor thing!"

— *Boston Transcript*

❌   ❌   ❌

Bishop Boodman (*impressively*) — "Only think, children! In Africa there are 10,000,000 square miles of territory without a single Sunday school where little boys and girls can spend their Sundays. Now, what should we all try and save up our money and do?"

Class (*in ecstatic union*) — "Go to Africa!"

— *Tid-Bits*

❌   ❌   ❌

Missionary — "Why do you look at me so intently?"

Cannibal — "I am the food inspector."

— *Buffalo Commercial*

First Cannibal — "The chief has hay fever."

Second Cannibal — "Serves him right; we warned him not to eat the grass widow."

— Awgwan

✠   ✠   ✠

The task of missionaries is much easier in lands where the people can't read about white civilization.

— Publishers Syndicate (Chi.)

✠   ✠   ✠

Missionary — "And do you know nothing whatever of religion?"

Cannibal — "Well, we got a taste of it when the last missionary was here."

— Toledo Blade

✠   ✠   ✠

Rich Man — "No, sir. I'm sorry I cannot help you. I disapprove of foreign missions."

Returned Missionary — "But the scriptures command us to feed the hungry."

Rich Man — "Very likely. But we surely can feed them on something cheaper than missionaries."

✠   ✠   ✠

We have it from an eminent explorer that cannibals are very proud of their table manners. They always take the clergy with a grain of salt.

— Eve (London)

✠   ✠   ✠

If there is holiness in a beard then no one would be holier than a goat.

— St. Jerome

Names

Fingering through the large volume that is entitled *The Official Catholic Directory of 1932,* which contains the names of all members of the clergy in the United States, a priest made some interesting discoveries with regard to the names of those who have given their lives to the Church.

It was found, for instance, that there were seventeen American Presidents represented there with their names. The name of Father Richard Washington, pastor at Old Point Comfort, Va., who is a collateral descendant of the Father of Our Country, is there toward the end of nearly 20,000 names. There are priests whose last name is Adams, Arthur; seven Fathers Grant; 64 Fathers Hayes; then there are Fathers Harrison, Hoover, Harding, Jackson, Johnson, McKinley, Monroe, Pierce, Polk, Tyler; 15 Fathers Taylor and eighteen Fathers Wilson.

There is about every name among the priests in our country found among the names of the Old Testament and even the New. In the Davenport Diocese there is a Father Adam. The directory contains more than 40 Fathers Kane and there are Fathers Abel in Colorado, Indiana, and Michigan. There are two Fathers Abraham. In Carlisle, Kentucky, lives Father Jacob. Several priests bear the names of David, Sampson, and Daniel. Recalling the wisest of all men, we see Father Solomon with his charge out at Wilkes-Barre, Pennsylvania, and in the same state, at Shannon Castle, there is Father Aloysius Angel. Then, in Missouri, are Father Vater and Father Gott. Father Lord is at St. Louis University.

In order to build a church — Father Church belongs to the Syracuse diocese — you have to have something on which to build it. We have five Fathers Rock around the country at strategic points. Father Pope is pastor and prior at St. Dominic's Church in San Francisco. Skipping back to Champaign, Illinois, we find Father Cardinal. There are three Fathers Bishop and there are three Fathers Porter in New York, Cleveland, and Manchester, New Hampshire; four Fathers Dean; three Fathers Christian; out at Xavier College, in Cincinnati, there is Father Usher, which, of course, naturally reminds us of Father Cash up in the Buffalo diocese.

Amid all these priests there are, as there should be, many Graces; there are over twelve Fathers Grace. Then there are Matthew, Mark, Luke, and John numbered among the clergy.

Other names of good pastors and assistants are Father Temple and Father Tower and seven Fathers Bell.

In the spiritual life we are reminded of Father Abbey of Cleburne, Texas, two Fathers Abbott and Father Prior of Aurora, Illinois.

Innocent, Divine, Joy, Bliss, Love are marks of the Christian and the names of more priests. There is Father Priest at Cadiz, Ohio, and at Hazard, Kentucky, and Father Hope is at Notre Dame University. As every priest should give his blessing before leaving our company we ask all the above to do so. That will please Monsignor Blessing up in Providence, Rhode Island.

—N.C.W.C., 1933

❋   ❋   ❋

A professor of journalism in a Western university holds his right hand to heaven and his left on Holy Writ and swears that this is true: A reporter wrote an article in which he mentioned Mary Magdalene. The copy-desk man was irritated at the slovenly newspaper work of the reporter in not indicating in some way who Mary Magdalene was, and his irritation was increased when he looked her up in *Who's Who in America* and could not find her listed.

—R. Reid, *The Morality of the Newspaper* (Notre Dame, Ind., Press)

Oddities

The *Catholic Bookman* for December, 1937, informs its readers that Sister Mary James of Mt. St. Mary's College, Milwaukee, Wisconsin, won the tenth annual contest of the International Mark Twain Society for the best anecdote dealing with an author, an author either living or dead. Here it is:

One day during the World War, when G. K. Chesterton, who was a huge man weighing over 350 pounds, was walking along Fleet Street, London, he was accosted by a fanatic woman who asked indignantly:

"Why aren't you at the front?"

"Madam," replied Chesterton, "if you'll go around to the side and look at me, you'll see that I am out at the front."

— *The Sign*

❌   ❌   ❌

The tourist who had secured a guide within a few moments after his arrival in Rome spoke crisply to the man. "I've only got an hour or so to spare for Rome," said he, "and I want to see just two things — one's St. Peter's and the other is the Forum. Take me to them both as quick as you can."

The guide engaged a carriage into which the tourist jumped, and after a few words from the guide to the driver, the equipage started off at a brisk rate. Suddenly it stopped, and the tourist ceased his fire of questions abruptly.

"Hop out," said he to his guide, urging him by a slight push. "Now which is this, the Forum or St. Peter's?"

— *Youth's Companion*

❌   ❌   ❌

Cop Plays St. Pat: Rids Banana Car of Snakes With Shot Gun.
— Springfield, Mass., *Paper*

ALMOST WHOLLY HOLY

You may have to take a microscope to find some of the below-mentioned places on your map, but you'll find them, even if hidden back of a mountain.

Pope, North Carolina
Rome, New York
Bishop, California
Canon, Georgia
Chancellor, South Dakota
Rector, Illinois
Priest, Idaho
Dean, Colorado
Parsons, Kansas
Abbott, Nebraska
Friar Point, Mississippi
Deacons, New Jersey
St. Augustine, Florida
St. Albans, Vermont
St. Mary's, Pennsylvania
St. Helens, Oregon
St. John, Washington
St. Charles, Arkansas
St. Paul, Minnesota
St. Patrick, Missouri
Providence, Rhode Island
Sacred Heart, Oklahoma
Palestine, Alabama
Paradise Valley, Nevada

Eden, Utah
Bethany, Connecticut
Marquette, Michigan
Judith Gap, Montana
Santa Fe, New Mexico
Jordan, Indiana
Temple, New Hampshire
Church, Iowa
Chapel, Maryland
Mission, Delaware
Pulpit Harbor, Maine
Trappist, Kentucky
Jesuit Bend, Louisiana
Grace City, North Dakota
Blessings, Ohio
Angelus, South Carolina
Crossville, Tennessee
Novice, Texas
Christ Church, Virginia
Christmas, Arizona
Three Churches, West Virginia
Holy Hill, Wisconsin
Devils Tower, Montana
Corpus Christi, Texas

NOTE: Where is Massachusetts in this array of states? Well, just abbreviate it and you have MASS.

Anagram — "What is Christianity?" "It is Charity."

A rich man once came to John Bright, the famous English statesman, and said, "Mr. Bright, do you know that I am worth a million dollars?"

"Yes," said Bright, "I know you are and that is *all* you are worth."

�   �   ✖

An Evangelist is one who brings the gossip.
A martyr is a pile of wood set on fire with a man on top.
Possession by spirits means feeling like the devil.
Vulgate pertained to the amount of land granted by a lord to his villeins.
Martin Luther was arrested for selling indulgences in the streets of Rome without a license.

— From *More Boners**

✖   ✖   ✖

"WHAT THE IRISH KNOW ABOUT NOTHING"

This above sign was on an eastern church for St. Patrick's Day address. When the faithful from the auld sod came wondering what it would be about, they discovered it was snakes.

✖   ✖   ✖

I have some excuses to offer for the race to which I belong. My first excuse is that it is not a very good world to raise folks in anyway. It is not very well adapted for raising a magnificent people. There is only a quarter of it land to start with. It is three times better for raising fish than people: and in that one quarter there is not a tenth part of it fit for raising people.

— *Bob Ingersoll*

✖   ✖   ✖

"The Lord knows how Binks made his money!"
"No wonder he always looks worried."

— *St. Louis Globe-Democrat*

---

* Copyright, 1931, by the Viking Press, Inc., New York.

Adam and Abel were out walking one day after the Fall and passing by a heavily barred gate, Abel noticed the beautiful birds, beasts, flowing fountains, and majestic streams winding in the forbidden enclosure. "Father," asked the youthful pedestrian, "what is that beautiful place?" "That, son," said Adam, "is the place where your mother ate us out of house and home."

☒   ☒   ☒

Found in a monastery was this curious old bill, made out evidently by an artist for repainting and repairing a scriptural group:

"For correcting and varnishing the Ten Commandments, 5 flor.; for adorning Pontius Pilate and putting a new ribbon in his cap, 3 flor.; for refastening the Good Thief to his cross and giving him a new finger, 4 flor.; for replating and regilding the left wing of the Angel Gabriel, 4 flor.; for washing the servant of the high priest Caiphas, and putting crimson on his cheeks, 5 flor.; for renewing the sky, adding two stars, gilding the sun and cleaning the moon, 7 flor.; for retrimming Herod's robe, replacing his teeth, and straightening his wig, 2 flor.; for putting a pebble in David's sling, enlarging Goliath's head, and pasting his legs, 3 flor.; for covering Noah's Ark with pitch, 6 flor.; for piecing the shirt of the Prodigal Son and putting water in the swine's trough, 3 flor.; for putting a handle on the Samaritan's jug, 3 flor. — Total 45 flor."

☒   ☒   ☒

"There are no flies on Father Time" — as someone has said — "But time is always on the fly."

☒   ☒   ☒

E is the most fortunate and unfortunate letter. It is the beginning of existence, the end of trouble. It is always out of cash, always in debt, never out of danger. It is the center of honesty, though it starts off in error.

When there was much jesting over the fact that such sterling Hibernian names as Sovoldi, Metzger, Carrideo, and Karr adorned the Notre Dame football roster, a *New York Times* reporter suggested to Rockne by way of a defensive explanation, a slight change in the Latin quotation, *Non omnes moriar*. This reporter urged Rockne to reply, *Non omnes Moriaritys*. "Rock," it is said, roared at this suggestion.

✠   ✠   ✠

It is said that the great scientist, Ampere, was so absent-minded, that on the evening of a rainy day, he would come home, put his umbrella to bed and stretch himself out on the floor to dry.

✠   ✠   ✠

Some think the communists are dumb. Well, they aren't. They're well-Red.

— *Farley (Ia.) Advertiser*

✠   ✠   ✠

FOR TEMPUS FUGITTERBUGS
When as a babe I laughed and wept,
        Time crept.
When as a boy I dreamed and talked,
        Time walked.
When I became a full-fledged man,
        Time ran.
When as a man I older grew,
        Time flew.
Soon I shall find as the years pass on,
        Time gone!
And my Eternity begun:
        Time done.
Oh, Jesus, Lord: save me ere then!
        Amen.

— *D. W. in The Tablet* (London)

Pests

Father criticized the sermon, Mother the organist, the daughter thought the singing atrocious; Sonnie piped up, "I think it was a good show for a nickel."

�   ✕   ✕

A Chicago minister who said the Bible was "inspiring, but not inspired" is now resigning though not resigned.

— *Dallas News*

✕   ✕   ✕

Oh, it's possible that you may disagree with me on some minor points of doctrine. That's your blessed privilege and I wouldn't deprive you of it if I had the power. A pompous old fellow once called at the office of my religious monthly to inform me that I was radically wrong on every possible question. He seemed to think I had committed an unpardonable crime in daring to differ with him. I asked him to be seated and whistled for the devil — the printer's devil, the only kind we keep in the office of the *Iconoclast,* I told him to procure for me a six-shooter, a sledge hammer, and a boat. My visitor became greatly alarmed.

"Wh-what are you g-going to do?"

"Do?" I replied, "I'm going to shoot the printers, smash the press, and throw the type into the river. What in the name of the great Sanhedrin is the use of me printing the paper if I can't please you?"

— *Wm. C. Brann*

✕   ✕   ✕

A minister said to his banker, "What am I to do, for people bother me with the frequency of their visits to such a degree that their conversations produce a great distraction of my valuable time." The banker replied, "To everyone who is poor, lend; and from everyone who is rich, borrow. They'll soon discontinue their visits."

※　　　　※　　　　※

That's the price you pay when you WILL write, when you must write to be content. It's good fun really as long as you are young and vigorous. But oh, kind Heaven, when you're getting old, and your nerves are aging faster than the rest of you — then look out! You need a strong stomach to digest the publicity that the press agent will broadcast about you. You require nerves of brass to endure the gate-crashing crowd who will trap you somehow. And as a priest you mustn't duck from people as lay-men may. And nerves affect the stomach. And the stomach affects the temper. And you'll very likely go to your grave un-wept, unhonored, though not unsung, by your congregation who sigh with relief: "Yes, we miss him — in a way. But God bless us didn't he become an awful grouch?"

— *Rev. Will W. Whalen*

※　　　　※　　　　※

Why are some ministers worse than Brigham Young?

Because they have married more women than they can sup-port, and would like to marry more.

Politics

Three men, a physician, an engineer, and a politician, were discussing which of their professions was the oldest. The surgeon insisted that his had the right to that title. Didn't the Bible relate in Genesis how Eve had been made from Adam's rib, and wasn't that a medico's job, he inquired. The engineer disagreed with him. Earlier than that the Bible said that order had been brought out of chaos, he pointed out. That surely was an engineer's job. At that point the politician spoke up:

"Well, who do you suppose was responsible for the chaos?" he inquired pointedly.

✖   ✖   ✖

"I see where a clergyman running for office in Ohio was caught attempting to extort a bribe. This is a sad illustration of a clergyman in politics."

Zounds — "O no, it is a sad illustration of politics in a clergyman."

✖   ✖   ✖

Our pastor says that he is unalterably opposed to religion in politics and will never vote for anyone but a Protestant.

— *Columbus, Ohio, Journal*

✖   ✖   ✖

A clergyman says he always puts on his hat when he votes. It's more important, though, to put on one's thinking cap.

— *New York Post*

✖   ✖   ✖

What is man? Man is a creature of superior intelligence who elects creatures of inferior intelligence to govern him.

— *Columbia Record*

100

A little boy was crossing a shaky bridge on a dark night. His mother had often told him to pray in time of danger.

"God is good," said the urchin. "And the devil isn't bad either."

⚜   ⚜   ⚜

He was a candidate for senatorial honors, and was scheduled to speak in a small town. Anxious to discover the religious affiliation of the majority of his audience, he addressed them in this manner:

"My great-grandfather was an Episcopalian (silence) but my great-grandmother belonged to the Presbyterian church (more silence). My grandfather was a Baptist (silence) but my grandmother was a Duck River Baptist (loud applause) and I followed my grandmother!"

⚜   ⚜   ⚜

Tommy — "Pa, what does this paper mean by practical Christianity?"

Pa — "Practical Christianity, son, means that it does not interfere with a man's business."

⚜   ⚜   ⚜

When the German Emperor visited Pope Leo XIII, Count Bismarck tried to follow into the audience chamber. A gentleman of the Papal Court motioned to him to stand back, as there must be no third person at the interview.

"I am Count Herbert Bismarck," shouted the German, as he struggled to follow his master.

"That," replied the Roman with calm dignity, "accounts for, but does not excuse, your conduct."

⚜   ⚜   ⚜

Good political shepherds can get along without crooks.
— *Wall Street Journal*

The idea behind Communism is that the rest of the world will become as bad as Russia and then Russia will be as good as any other country.

※   ※   ※

Success? I would rather be a fox and steal fat geese than a miserly millionaire and prey upon the misfortunes of my fellows. I would rather be a doodle-bug burrowing in the dust than a plotting politician, trying to inflate a second-term gubernatorial boom with fetid breath of a foul hypocrisy. I would rather be a peddler of hot peanuts than a president who gives to bond-grabbers and boodlers privileges to despoil the pantries of the poor. I would rather play a cornstalk fiddle while pickaninnies dance, than build, of orphan's tears and widow's sighs, a flimsy bubble of fame to be blown adown the beach of time into Eternity's shoreless sea.

— Wm. C. Brann

Prayer

"You heard me say my prayers last night didn't you, nurse?"
"Yes, dear."
"And you heard me ask God to make me a good girl?"
"Yes."
"Well, He didn't do it."

※   ※   ※

Act I — "Heaven, send us help to save the crop."
Act II — "Too much crop. Government help us."
— *Memphis News-Scimiter*

※   ※   ※

Sunday-School Teacher — "Dear children, tell me the last thing you do before you go to bed."
Wise Child — "Park the door key in the mailbox for grandma."

※   ※   ※

A farmer whose barn was full of corn was accustomed to pray that the wants of the poor might be supplied; but when anybody in needy circumstances asked him for some of his corn, he said he had none to spare. One day after his son had heard him pray for the poor and needy he said to him, "Father, I wish I had your corn."
"Why, my son, what would you do with it?"
"I would answer your prayers right away," replied the son.

※   ※   ※

Asked to pray for warm weather so that her grandma's rheumatism might pass away, a five-year-old girl knelt and said:
"Oh, Lord, please make it hot for grandma."

AN EVERYDAY MAN'S PRAYER

Teach me that sixty minutes make an hour, sixteen ounces one pound, and one hundred cents one dollar.

Help me to so live that I can lie down at night with a clear conscience, without a gun under my pillow, and unhaunted by the faces of those to whom I have brought pain.

Grant that I may earn my meal ticket on the square and in earning it may do unto others as I would have them do unto me.

Deafen me to the jingle of tainted money; blind me to the faults of the other fellow, but reveal to me my own.

Guide me that so each night when I look across the table at my dear wife, who has been a blessing to me, I will have nothing to conceal.

Keep me young enough to laugh with little children, and sympathetic enough to be considerate of old age.

And when comes the day of darkened shades, and the smell of flowers, the tread of soft footsteps, and the crunching of wheels in the yard — make the ceremony short and the inscription on the tombstone simply:

HERE LIES A MAN

— *Author Unknown*

❈   ❈   ❈

Visitor — "What does the chaplain do here?"

Freshman — "Oh, he gets up in chapel every morning, looks over the student body, and then prays for the college."

— *Lehigh Burr*

❈   ❈   ❈

Mother — "Have you said your prayers, Bobby?"

Bobby — "Yes, Mother."

Mother — "And did you ask God to make you a good boy?"

Bobby — "Yes, Mother — but not yet."

— *Sydney Bulletin*

Her Excuse — A tiny four-year-old was spending a night away from home. At bedtime she knelt at the knee of her hostess to say her prayers, expecting the usual prompting. Finding Mrs. Beak unable to help her out, she concluded thus:

"Please, God, 'scuse me. I can't remember my prayers, and I'm staying with a lady who don't know any."

— *Home Herald*

❌ ❌ ❌

OREMUS

One need not kneel within the dim-lit nave
  Of some cathedral with its towering spire
To offer up a prayer that will be heard
  In heavenly realms where sing the angels' choir.

One need not steal away from all the throng
  And kneel within the forest's deepest heart
To make a prayer that will ascend on high,
  Becoming of celestial things a part.

Prayers need not even form themselves in words
  Or holy phrases; each small act we do,
Each kindly thought, each friendly, helpful gesture
  May turn into a prayer for me or you.

Going your daily way, then, you are praying
  If God is in your heart and welcomed there;
Nothing in His name is ever lowly —
  Wiping up a floor may be a prayer.

— Jazbo of Old Dubuque in *Chicago Tribune*

❌ ❌ ❌

"Well, darling, what did you see at church today?" a little three-year-old was asked after her first visit to a real church service. "Oh, Muvver, I saw de funniest thing — dere was a man dat said his prayers and den he didn't go to bed."

— *Chicago Daily News*

✒   ✒   ✒

"We'd have more prayers answered," said a Bishop, "if we had more faith.

"Too many of us are like Willie. Willie, on a visit to his uncle's in the country, admired a fine colt.

"'Uncle, give me that colt, will you?' he asked.

"'Why, no, Willie,' said his uncle, 'That's a very valuable colt, and I couldn't afford to give him to you. Do you want a colt so very badly?'

"'I'd rather have a colt than anything else in the world,' said Willie.

"'Then,' said his uncle, 'I'll tell you what you ought to do. Since you want a colt that much, you ought to pray for one. Whenever I want a thing I always pray for it, and then it is sure to come to me.'

"'Is that so, uncle?' said Willie, eagerly. 'Won't you please give me this colt, then, and pray for one for yourself?'"

— *Pittsburgh Chron-Tel.*

✒   ✒   ✒

A little fellow was learning from his aunt about Grant, Lee, and other famous leaders of the Civil War. "Is that the same Grant we pray to in church?" he inquired innocently.

"Pray to in church? You are mistaken, dear," said the aunt.

"No, I'm not," he insisted, "For during service we always say, 'Grant, we beseech Thee, to hear us.'"

— *Boston Transcript*

✒   ✒   ✒

A bright little girl, aged four, and her brother, aged six, were spending the night with their aunt. When bedtime came the aunt asked them how they said their prayers. The little girl answered:

"Sometimes I say them on muddy's knees and sometimes to the side of the bed."

"And how about you, little boy?" asked the aunt.

"Oh, I don't need to pray. I sleep with daddy."

— Everybody's Magazine

✖   ✖   ✖

It was down in the bloody hills of Kentucky. A terrific storm came up suddenly while a religious colored parson was returning home on his mule. Roaring thunder was to be heard on all sides while only an occasional flash of lightning showed the traveler the uncertain road. Finally he made this little prayer, "O Lord, if it is all the same to You I'd like to have a little less noise and a little more light."

✖   ✖   ✖

Prayer of a Scotch preacher — "Oh, Lord, guide us aright for we are verra, verra determined."

✖   ✖   ✖

May the blessing of God await thee. May the sun of glory shine around thy bed; and may the gates of plenty, honor and happiness be ever open to thee. May no sorrow distress thy days; may no grief disturb thy nights. May the pillow of peace kiss thy cheek, and the pleasures of imagination attend thy dreams; and when length of years makes thee tired of earthly joys and the curtain of death gently closes round thy last sleep of human existence, may the Angel of God attend thy bed, and take care that the expiring lamp of life shall not receive one rude blast to hasten on its extinction.

— Charles Dickens

✖   ✖   ✖

Modern Youngster — Prayers are little messages to God, sent at night to get the cheaper rate.

A bishop was traveling in the "Isle of Man." Passing a crowd of convicts who were breaking rock, he stopped the carriage and began conversing with the convicts. "Oh," he exclaimed, "if I could break the stony hearts of men as easily as you break those stones!"

"Your lordship," quietly asked one, "do you ever try working on your knees?"

※   ※   ※

"Papa, is God dead?"

"No, my dear. Why do you ask?"

" 'Cause, Papa, you never talk to Him anymore at night like you used to."

※   ※   ※

These quaint old words were an old time grace,
"He that without grace sitteth down to eate,
Forgetting to Give God thanks for his meate,
And rising againe, letting Grace overpasse,
Sittest down like an oxe and riseth like an asse."

※   ※   ※

"Dear God," prayed golden-haired Willie, "please watch over my mamma."

And then he added as an afterthought, "And I dunno as it would do any harm to keep an eye on dad, too."

※   ※   ※

A celebrated revivalist came to address his flock, and before he began to speak the pastor said: "Brother Jones, before you begins this discourse, there is some powerful bad Negroes in this here congregation, and I want to pray for you," which he did in this fashion:

"O Lord, give Brother Jones the eye of the eagle, that he may see sin from afar. Glue his ear to the gospel telephone, and connect him with the central skies. Illuminate his brow with a brightness that will make the fires of hell look like a tallow candle. Nail his hands to the gospel plow, and bow his head in some lonesome valley where prayer is much wanted to be said, and anoint him all over with the kerosene oil of Thy salvation and set him afire."

— *Congressional Records*

AN INVOCATION

"Lord of all pots and pans and things,
Since I have not time to be a saint by doing lovely things;
And watching late with Thee, or dreaming in the twilight,
   or storming Heaven's gate
Make me a saint by getting meals or washing up the plates.

"Although I must have Martha's hands, I have a Mary mind,
And when I black the boots or shoes, Thy sandals, Lord,
   I find.
I think of how You trod the earth each time I scrub the
   floor
Accept this meditation, Lord, I haven't time for more.

"Warm all the kitchen with Thy Love and light it with
   Thy peace,
Forgive me all my worrying and make all grumbling cease.
Thou who didst love to give men food, in room or by the
   sea,
Accept this service that I do — I do it all for Thee."

— *Cecily Hallack*

       ❈   ❈   ❈

A little four-year-old knelt beside her bed and after repeating, "Now I lay me down to sleep," added, "Please take care of papa, and auntie, God, and take care of Yourself, too."

The story is told of St. Bernard that one day, riding a horse, he met a peasant. The peasant asked him why he was so wrapt in thought. "I'm trying to pray without distraction," said the Saint.

"I never have distractions at prayer," said the peasant.

"If you can say the 'Our Father' without a distraction, I'll give you this horse."

The peasant began, "Our Father — " and when he got to "lead us not into temptation," he hesitated and looked up into Bernard's face saying, "Will you give me the saddle, too?"

      ✄   ✄   ✄

Little Girl's Prayer — "O God, make all the bad people good and all the good people nice."

      ✄   ✄   ✄

Little Dorothy in a Catholic church for the first time, asked her mother, "What are they going to do now?"

"Say their prayers," said the mother.

"With all their clothes on?" asked Dorothy in surprise.

      ✄   ✄   ✄

Some boys were taunting a poor barefooted lad one day, making fun of his Christian faith. They said to him, "If God really loves you, why doesn't He take better care of you, why doesn't He tell somebody to send you a pair of shoes?"

The lad seemed puzzled for a moment, then with tears rushing to his eyes, replied, "I think He does tell people, but they are not listening."

— *Catholic Missions*

Religion

It looks now as if the Southern and Northern Methodists won't get together until they get to Heaven.

— Dallas News

𝕯   𝕯   𝕯

Someone has said that "If we could get religion like a Baptist, experience it like a Methodist, be positive about it like a Catholic, be proud of it like an Episcopalian, pay for it like a Presbyterian, propagate it like an Adventist, and enjoy it like a Negro — that would be some religion."

𝕯   𝕯   𝕯

Father O'Brien and Rabbi Benjamin were fast friends, despite differences in religion. At a banquet, they were seated at a table when an especially delicious dish of ham was passed around, and Father O'Brien commented on the fine flavor. Then he leaned over and asked the Rabbi when he was going to begin eating ham.

"At your wedding," twitted the Rabbi.

𝕯   𝕯   𝕯

There's this to be said in favor of Mormonism: it doesn't throw the entire burden of supporting a husband on one woman.

— Roanoke Times

𝕯   𝕯   𝕯

Christian-Science Mamma — "He must imagine he has the colic."

Christian-Science Papa — "I wish he'd imagine I'm walking the floor with him."

— Puck

111

"She devoted her life to Christian Science."
"Indeed. What did she die of?"

— *Brooklyn Life*

♛   ♛   ♛

The widow trying to get in touch with her deceased husband, sat patiently while the spiritualist struggled vainly for over half an hour. Finally, in despair, the medium said:

"I'm afraid the conditions are not favorable tonight, madame. I can't seem to establish communication with Mr. Smith."

"Oh, well, I'm not surprised," said the widow, glancing at the clock. "I see it's only eight thirty and he rarely ever showed up until after 1 a.m."

♛   ♛   ♛

A lady was asked why she came so early to church. "Because it is my religion never to disturb the religion of other people."

♛   ♛   ♛

A certain preacher having changed his religion, was much blamed by his friends for deserting them. To excuse himself, he said, "I have reasons." Asked what they were, he replied, "A wife and six children."

♛   ♛   ♛

If religion and science quarrel it is because we have neither religion enough nor science enough.

— *Burlington Hawk-Eye*

♛   ♛   ♛

These Paris, Illinois, folks have no connection, but they are all here: Parish, Church, Pugh, Bell, Sexton, Singer, Elder, Deacon, Goodpastor, Bishop, Neal, Mark, Luke, and James. They have the Mean and Money to carry on, but no congregation. The "Lord" who once dwelt among them left several years ago.

— *Chicago Tribune*

"Do you belong to the Law and Order society?"
"Yes, sir, got anybody you want lynched?"

— Atlanta Constitution

❊   ❊   ❊

Chinese Doctor's Ad: Insertion of false teeth and eyes, latest methodists.

❊   ❊   ❊

To the great god Buddha came the representatives of the Catholic, Protestant, and Jewish religions, to pay him homage. Buddha, very flattered told each of them that if they would express a wish, it would be fulfilled.

"What do you wish?" he asked the Catholic.

The answer was "Glory."

"You shall have it," said Buddha, and turning to the Protestant, "What do you wish?"

"Money."

"You shall have it."

"And you?" this to the Jew.

"I do not want much," quoth he, "give me the Protestant's address!"

— Pall Mall Gazette

❊   ❊   ❊

A Negro was telling his minister that he had "got Religion."

"Dat's fine, brothah; but is you sure you is going to lay aside sin?" asked the minister.

"Yessuh, Ah's done it already."

"An' is you gwine to pay up all yoh debts?"

"Wait a minute, Pahson! You ain't talkin' religion now — you is talking business!"

❊   ❊   ❊

Of all the riches that we hug, of all the pleasures we enjoy, we carry no more out of this world than out of a dream.

— Bonnell

A Mormon once argued polygamy with Mark Twain. The Mormon insisted that polygamy was moral, and he defied Twain to cite any passage of Scripture that forbade the practice.

"Well," said the humorist, "how about that passage that tells us no man can serve two masters?"

— *The Argonaut*

❈   ❈   ❈

The Christian Scientist — "Sickness is only a manifestation of sin."

The Regular Practitioner — "Then, madame, your husband is on the road to perdition."

❈   ❈   ❈

Old Lady (*offering policeman a tract*) — "I often think you poor policemen run such a risk of becoming bad, being so constantly mixed up with crime."

Policeman — "You needn't fear, mum. It's the criminals wot runs the risks of becomin' saints, bein' mixt up with us!"

— *Punch*

❈   ❈   ❈

What this country needs is dirtier fingernails and cleaner minds.

— *Will Rogers*

❈   ❈   ❈

A bishop was being patronized by a millionaire.

"I never go to church, Bishop," the millionaire said, "there are too many hypocrites there."

"Oh, don't let that keep you away," said the Bishop smiling. "There's always room for one more, you know."

❈   ❈   ❈

It is about as hard for a rich man to enter Heaven as it is for a poor man to remain upon earth.

— *New Orleans Times-Picayune*

A priest offered 25 cents to the boy who could tell him who was the greatest man in history.

"Christopher Columbus," answered the Italian boy.

"George Washington," answered the American lad.

"St. Patrick," shouted the Jewish boy.

"The quarter is yours," said the priest, "but why did you say St. Patrick?"

"Right down in my heart I knew it was Moses," said the Jewish boy, "but business is business."

— Exchange

☒ ☒ ☒

Mike — "Did you see this here where one of the Bishops of Ireland has turned Communist?"

Molly — "I didn't."

Mike — "Indade, it's true. He's getting a Red Hat."

☒ ☒ ☒

On a certain Sunday morning the pastor noticed a new attendant at the church.

When the meeting was over the preacher made it his business to speak to the newcomer.

"Erastus," he said, "this is the first time I have seen you at church for a long time. I'm mighty glad to see you here."

"I had to come," replied Rastus, "I needs strengthenin', I'se got a job whitewashin' a chicken coop and buildin' a fence around a watermelon patch."

— N.Y.C. Lines Magazine

☒ ☒ ☒

The college student, son of a clergyman, discovered he was uncomfortably short of money, so he spent some time concocting a letter which should have the right effect upon a somewhat severe and pious parent. When finally completed, the letter read:

"My dear Father: I wonder if you will oblige me very greatly by sending me a copy of this month's Parish Magazine, also $50. P.S. Don't forget the Parish Magazine."

— Cincinnati Enquirer

✄   ✄   ✄

One day a rich but miserly man came to a rabbi. The rabbi led him to a window and told him to look outside.

"What do you see?" asked the rabbi.

"People," answered the rich miser.

Then the rabbi led him to a mirror and asked: "What do you see now?"

"I see myself," was the answer.

The rabbi said: "Behold, in the window there is glass, and in the mirror there is glass. But the glass of the mirror is covered with a little silver, and no sooner is a little silver added than you cease to see others and see only yourself."

— Our Sunday Visitor

✄   ✄   ✄

"Have you got 'The Life of a Christian' here?" asked the customer of a bookseller's assistant.

"The life of a Christian?" replied the harassed youth. "Lady, I haven't the life of a dog."

— The Witness

✄   ✄   ✄

The *London Universe* tells the story of a priest in a remote district who had to say Masses on Sunday in churches a long distance apart. Arriving at the distant church he was vexed to find that he had forgotten the key to the front door, but one of the congregation volunteered to say the Rosary for the congregation until he should return with the key. He was gone a long time — much longer than he had expected — and when he came back he found that the volunteer was announcing the sixtieth decade of the Rosary, for which he had suggested for the meditation, "The Stabbing of Pontius Pilate by Judas Iscariot."

Three hermits went out and lived in a cave, promising to keep eternal silence. After several years one of the boys saw a cow that reminded him of his youth.

"I am reminded of the days of old," said he.

A year passed and one of the other hermits said, "So am I."

Another year passed and the third hermit said, "If you two can't keep silence, I'm going to leave."

— *Catholic Daily Tribune*

      ❊   ❊   ❊

Every day in every way our newspapermen appear to know less and less about religion. I cannot vouch for this story but it illustrates the point. There was a strike of coal miners somewhere not far from the Ohio River Valley and a staff man from a metropolitan newspaper was sent to cover it. He started his story in a flamboyant manner, writing impressively, "Jehovah is with the miners in the mountains tonight." When the story was wired in, the managing editor glanced through the first paragraph, and then wired back, "Interview Jehovah and send five hundred words."

— R. Reid, *The Morality of the Newspaper* (Notre Dame, Ind., Press)

      ❊   ❊   ❊

You are writing a gospel,
    A chapter each day
By the deeds that you do
    And the words that you say.

Men read what you write
    Whether faithless or true.
Say! What is the gospel
    According to you?

— *Paul Gilbert*

Sermons

A minister down in the Ozarks boasted that he had talked to his congregation for an hour and a half.

"Weren't you tired afterwards?" asked a neighboring minister.

"No, but the congregation was," said the marathon preacher.

✝   ✝   ✝

This little story comes from the South.

The first slice of goose had been cut, and the Negro minister, who had been invited to dine, looked at it with as keen anticipation as was displayed in the faces around him.

"Dat's as fine a goose as I ever saw, Brudder Williams," he said to his host. "Where did you get such a fine one?"

"Well, now, Mistah Rawley," said the carver of the goose with a sudden access of dignity, "when you preach a special good sermon I never axes you wh're you got it. Seems to me dat's a triv'al matter, anyway."

— Philadelphia Ledger

✝   ✝   ✝

A joke unconsciously perpetrated by the vicar of St. John's ought to rank high in the annals of pulpit humor. Before the service started the vicar was handed a lady's watch which had been found in the churchyard. After making the customary announcements, says the *North Mail,* he referred to the finding of the watch, which, he stated, was in the vestry awaiting an owner, and then solemnly said, "Hymn No. 110: Lord, her watch Thy church is keeping."

— Christian Register

✝   ✝   ✝

Wendell Phillips, according to a biography by Dr. Lorenzo

Sears, was, on one occasion lecturing in Ohio, and while on a railroad journey, going to keep one of his appointments, he met in the car a crowd of clergy, returning from some sort of convention. One of the ministers felt called upon to approach Mr. Phillips and asked him: "Are you Mr. Phillips?"

"I am, sir."

"Are you trying to free the niggers?"

"Yes, sir; I am an abolitionist."

"Well, why do you preach your doctrines up here? Why don't you go over into Kentucky?"

"Excuse me, are you a preacher?"

"I am, sir."

"Are you trying to save souls from hell?"

"Yes, sir; that's my business."

"Well, why don't you go there?"

❈   ❈   ❈

A woman's preaching is like a dog walking on his hind legs. It is not done well, but you are surprised to find it done at all.

— *Samuel Johnson*

❈   ❈   ❈

Archbishop Downey of Liverpool, England, has made these three rules for preaching:

"Remember the longer the spoke the bigger the tire."

"If a man cannot strike oil in ten minutes he ought to stop boring."

"Be bright, be brief, and be gone."

❈   ❈   ❈

A member of the cloth mounted the pulpit with a great air of importance. In the midst of the sermon, he broke down, forgot his manuscript, and was forced to come down dejected.

One of his clerical friends remarked to him: "If you went up as you came down, you would have come down as you went up."

"De preacher wuzn't feelin' good las' meetin' day, and he made de stove preach de sermon."

"Made de stove preach?"

"Yes — made it red hot fum top ter bottom an' den tol' de sinners ter take a good look at it, an' get ter thinkin'."

— Atlanta Constitution

�   ✱   ✱

The services in the chapel of a certain Western university are from time to time conducted by eminent clergymen of many denominations and from many cities.

On one occasion, when one of these visiting divines asked the president of the university how long he should speak, that witty officer replied: "There is no limit, doctor, upon the time you may preach; but I may tell you that there is a tradition here that the most souls are saved during the first twenty minutes."

— Lippincott's

✱   ✱   ✱

New Vicar — "Are people subject to colds in these parts? Quite a lot of people coughed during my sermon."

Old Verger — "Coughs, sir — them ain't coughs them's time signals."

✱   ✱   ✱

"That certainly was a very fine sermon," said an enthusiastic church member who was an ardent admirer of the minister. "A fine sermon, and well-timed, too."

"Yes," answered his unadmiring neighbor, "it certainly was well-timed. Fully half of the congregation had their watches out."

— Watchman-Examiner

✱   ✱   ✱

"Everything considered he preaches a reasonably good sermon. It is hard to avoid offending people like us," said the top-hatted gentleman to his wife as he was leaving church.

Mark Twain went up to congratulate a priest after the services one Sunday. "It was a good sermon, Father," said the humorist, "and I have a book at home with every word of your sermon in it." "I'd like very much to see it," said the priest. "I'll be glad to send you the copy." Next day the priest received a dictionary from the author of *Tom Sawyer*.

❊   ❊   ❊

The minister called on Mrs. McShoddie: "By the way," he remarked, "I was sorry to see your husband leave the church Sunday night in the middle of my sermon. I trust nothing is seriously wrong with him?"

"Oh, no," replied the Mrs., "but you see the poor man has a terrible habit of walking in his sleep."

❊   ❊   ❊

There is a clergyman in Richmond, Virginia, who enjoys telling the following at his own expense: "One Sunday I was returning home when I was accosted by a quaint old woman, housekeeper in the employ of a dear friend of mine.

" 'I want to tell you, sir,' said the old woman, 'how much I enjoy going to church on the days that you preach.'

"Expressing my appreciation of the compliment, I added that I was much gratified to hear it, adding that I feared I was not as popular a minister as others in the city, and I finally asked: 'And what particular reason have you for enjoyment when I preach?'

" 'Oh, sir,' she answered with appalling candor, 'I get such a good seat then.' "

— Philadelphia Ledger

❊   ❊   ❊

"Do you think they approved of my sermon?" asked the newly appointed rector, hopeful that he had made a good impression.

"Yes, I think so," replied his wife. "They were all nodding."

— Pathfinder

The following is a bishop's description of the kind of preaching sometimes addressed to fashionable congregations: "Brethren unless you repent, in a measure, and be converted, as it were, you will, I regret to say, be damned to some extent."

✄   ✄   ✄

A southern Negro minister who was given to the use of big words and complicated discourse was waited upon by the church committee and told that his style of preaching was not all that could be desired.

"Don't I argify and sputify?" inquired the minister.

"Yes, yo' done argify and sputify," responded a member of the committee, "but yo' don't show wherein."

— *Boston Transcript*

✄   ✄   ✄

This is veracious: A clergyman from Cambridge, Massachusetts, had occasion to preach to the inmates of an insane hospital. During his sermon he noticed that one of the patients paid the closest attention, his eyes riveted upon the preacher's face, his body bent eagerly forward. Such interest was most flattering. After the service, the speaker noticed that the man spoke to the superintendent, so as soon as possible the preacher inquired, "Didn't that man speak to you about my sermon?"

"Yes."

"Would you mind telling me what he said?"

The superintendent tried to sidestep, but the preacher insisted.

"Well," he said at last, "what the man said was, 'Just think he's out and I'm in.'"

— *The Christian Register* (Boston)

✄   ✄   ✄

A belated churchgoer, arriving during the sermon on a recent Sunday, whispered to an Irish friend in front of him: "Isn't he finished yet?" With an edifying effort to control his feelings, the friend answered: "Through, is it? Sure, he's through long ago, but he wouldn't stop." Which reminds us of another apt reply made by an old pastor to a young curate, who asked how long a sermon should be. The deliberate answer was: "Well, if a sermon bears the slightest resemblance to Our Lord's Sermon on the Mount, it may be a short one. I have heard somewhere that if a sermon is good, it needn't be long, and if it isn't good, it ought to be short."

— Ave Maria

One day Cardinal Gibbons told Chief Justice Taney that he always felt a certain embarrassment when he saw the distinguished jurist in the Baltimore cathedral when he was preaching.

"I always," said Chief Justice Taney, "listen to the Lord's appointed with attention and reverence. I regard all sermons as good when Christ is extolled and virtue praised. Indeed, I never heard a bad sermon in my life."

In order to impress upon his congregation the length of eternity, a colored preacher used the following illustration: "If a sparrow, breddern, should take a drop of water from the Atlantic Ocean at Coney Island, and with this drop of water in his beak should hop a hop a day until it reached the Pacific Ocean at San Francisco, and when it got there should let the drop fall into the Pacific, and when this was done should turn around and hop a hop a day all the way back to Coney Island and get another drop and do the same thing over, and keep on doing this very same thing until it had carried the whole Atlantic Ocean over to the Pacific, it would then only be early morning in eternity."

We are with the ministers if they strike for better paid sermons unless they ask time and a half for overtime.

— Detroit News

A beadle had been laying a new carpet in the pulpit, and left a number of tacks on the floor.

"What do you suppose would happen if I stepped on one of those during the sermon?" asked the minister.

"Well, sir," replied the beadle, "that would be one point you would not linger on."

           ❈   ❈   ❈

Nothing preaches better than the ant and she says nothing.

— *Ben Franklin*

           ❈   ❈   ❈

Whenever a minister haz preached a sermon that pleazes the whole congregashun, he haz probably preached one that the Lord won't endorse.

— *Josh Billings*

           ❈   ❈   ❈

Two candidates for a pulpit in a small town were lodged in adjoining hotel rooms the night before their tryouts. Through the thin wall Preacher A heard Preacher B rehearsing his address. Recognizing it as superior to his own, he copied it word for word, knowing he was to speak first the following evening.

The next evening Preacher A delivered the stolen speech and received tumultuous applause. Then Preacher B got up. "I must confess," he said, "that I never heard such a marvelous speech. Knowing that I cannot improve upon it, I shall repeat it word for word." He did and it earned undying fame.

Sunday

Two Highland farmers met on their way to church. "Man," said Donald, "I was wonderin' what you will be askin' for yon bit sheep over at your steadin?"

"Man," replied Dougal, "I was thinkin' I wad be wantin' fifty shullin's for that sheep."

"I will tak' it at that," said Donald, "but och, man Dougal, I am awfu' surprised at you doin' business on the Sawbath."

"Business!" exclaimed Dougal. "Man, sellin' a sheep like that for fifty shullin's is not business at all; it's just charity."

— Ladies' Home Journal

✖   ✖   ✖

The Preacher — "Do you know where little boys go who fish on Sunday?"

The Kid — "Yes, sir; all us kids around here go down ter Smylies crick below the bridge." *— Brooklyn Life*

✖   ✖   ✖

"Lives of motorists remind us
On a Sunday afternoon
That some drive as if they'd like to
Try and end them pretty soon."

✖   ✖   ✖

Jack — "Why don't they allow jokes in the English theaters on Saturday evening?"

Jill — "So they won't be laughing in church on Sunday."

✖   ✖   ✖

Coming home on Sunday with a string of trout, Bobbie met the minister. Seeing he was in for it, Bobbie approached the minister and said, "See, minister, what the trout got for nibblin' worms on Sunday."

⋈ ⋈ ⋈

Rich Uncle — "I am extremely sorry to learn that Eustace is in the habit of visiting the golf club on the Sabbath."

Fond Father — "Oh, but he doesn't play. He only pops over there for a few drinks and a game of bridge."

⋈ ⋈ ⋈

"How long do you sleep on Sunday?"
"It all depends."
"On what?"
"The length of the sermon."

⋈ ⋈ ⋈

John Ruskin was always annoyed by inclement weather, but in the following statements he tells why a Christian should not remain away from church even on a rainy Sunday. Among them are these:

BECAUSE the Fourth Commandment does not except the rainy Lord's Day.

BECAUSE I may miss exactly the prayer or sermon I need.

BECAUSE the rain did not keep me from the tea last Monday, nor the dinner last Wednesday, nor the ball game last Saturday, nor the store any day in the week.

BECAUSE an example which cannot stand a little wetting is of little account.

BECAUSE my faith should not be a matter of thermometers.

BECAUSE the man who fears the rain, will soon fear the cloud, and he who fears the day will soon fear the daylight itself as reason for neglecting the church.

⋈ ⋈ ⋈

"Don't you know you will be punished for fishing on Sunday?" asked the shocked minister of the little boy on the river-bank.

"Not on your life!" replied the young angler. "Dad himself is fishing a little way down the stream."

— *Richmond Times-Dispatch*

✝   ✝   ✝

Foozle — "Do you think it wrong to play golf on Sunday?"

Niblick — "I think it wrong to play such a game as you do on any day of the week."

— *Boston Transcript*

✝   ✝   ✝

I spent a year in that town, one Sunday.

— *Warwick Deeping*

Sunday School

One of the good nuns who teaches in a Dubuque school was anxious to secure a calendar with a picture of the Quintuplets on it. One day she asked the little folks in her class if they could help her out. One little chap promptly raised his hand and when the Sister motioned him to speak, he arose and said, "We have one at home, but I don't think Mamma will let you have it: it covers up a big crack in the sittin' room wall."

— Jazbo of Old Dubuque

❈   ❈   ❈

Teacher — "What's Dick doing now?"
Willie — "Well, Dick is a cattle salesman."
Teacher — "And Harry?"
Willie — "He's a politician."
Teacher — "And Tom?"
Willie — "Tom's a minister."
Teacher — "And what's your father doing?"
Willie — "Oh, dad's farmin' and feeding Tom, Dick, and Harry."

❈   ❈   ❈

The minister was addressing the Sunday school. "Children, I want to talk to you for a few moments about one of the most wonderful, one of the most important organs in the whole world," he said. "What is it that throbs away, beats away, never stopping, never ceasing, whether you wake or sleep, night or day, week in and week out, month in and month out, year in and year out, without any violation on your part, hidden away in the depths, as it were unseen by you, throbbing, throbbing, throbbing, rhythmically all your life long?"

During this pause for oratorical effect a small voice was heard: "I know. It's the gas meter."

— Tid-Bits

During a quiz in a confirmation class, the bishop asked a small boy who made the world.

The youngster who was plainly quite nervous said, "I didn't."

�֍   ✖   ✖

"Now, boys," said the teacher in the juvenile Sunday-school class, "our lesson today teaches us that if we are good while here on earth, when we die we will go to a place of everlasting bliss. But suppose we are bad, then what will become of us?"

"We'll go to a place of everlasting blister," promptly answered the small boy at the pedal extremity of the class.

— *Brooklyn Citizen*

✖   ✖   ✖

"I told you last Sunday, children," said the Sunday-school teacher, "that you should try to make someone happy during the week. How many of you have done so?"

"I did," answered a boy promptly.

"That's nice, Johnny. What did you do?"

"I went to see my aunt and she's always happy when I go home."

— *Louisville Courier-Journal*

✖   ✖   ✖

"What happened to Babylon?" asked the Sunday-school teacher.

"It fell!" cried the pupil.

"And what became of Nineveh?"

"It was destroyed."

"And what of Tyre?"

"Punctured!"

— *Cleveland Leader*

✖   ✖   ✖

The Sunday-school teacher was talking to her pupils on patience. She explained her topic carefully, and as an aid to under-

standing she gave each pupil a card bearing the picture of a boy
fishing. "Even pleasure," she said, "requires the exercise of patience. See the boy fishing; he must sit down and wait. He must
be patient. And now can any little boy tell me what do we need
most when we go fishing?"

The answer was quickly shouted with one voice: "Bait!"

— *Selected*

✄   ✄   ✄

"Pa, did you go to Sunday school when you were a boy?"

"Yes, my son, I always went to Sunday school."

"Well, Dad, I think I'll quit going. It ain't doing me any good
either."

— *Menthology*

✄   ✄   ✄

"William," said the Sunday-school teacher, "can you tell me
what you must do before a sin can be forgiven?"

"Yes, sir," replied William, "we must sin!"

✄   ✄   ✄

The minister's class at the kirk of Tobermory had been reading the story of Joseph and his brethren and it came to the turn
of the minister to examine the boys.

The replies to all his questions had been quick, intelligent,
and correct. Such as:

"What great crime did these sons of Jacob commit?"

"They sold their brother Joseph."

"Quite correct. And for how much?"

"Twenty pieces of silver."

"And what added to the cruelty and wickedness of these bad
brothers?"

A pause. A little Highlander stretched out an eager hand.
"Well, my man?"

"Please, sir, they sell't him too cheap."

— *Tid-Bits*

Ten Commandments

Sunday-School Teacher — "Reginald, can you repeat the short-est commandment? It has but four words."
Reginald — "Keep off the grass!"

♢   ♢   ♢

"Moses," said Uncle Eben, "was a great lawgiver. But de way he was satisfied to keep the ten commandments short and to de point shows that he wasn't no regular lawyer."

— *Washington Evening Star*

♢   ♢   ♢

Johnny — "Did Moses have no illness like what you got?"
Dad — "How on earth do I know? Why do you ask such a question?"
Johnny — "Well, our Sunday-school teacher says the Lord gave Moses two tablets."

— *London Mail*

♢   ♢   ♢

"I see," said Hicks, "that they have started a movement over in England to remodel the Ten Commandments."
"Remodel, eh?" retorted Dickens. "What a waste of time — all they need is restoration."

— *Harper's Weekly*

♢   ♢   ♢

The Bible tells us to love our neighbors, and also to love our enemies; probably because they are generally the same people.

— *G. K. Chesterton*

♢   ♢   ♢

Honor thy father and mother, but not a stranger's check.

Roger W. Babson, the statistician, tells us that he once sent to his customers a leaflet, "Essentials of Business Success." He simply printed the Ten Commandments, and Christ's new law of love. From one correspondent he received the enthusiastic reply: "I have never seen such a fine statement of essentials. Where did you get it?"

✠   ✠   ✠

"In vain we call old notions fudge
And bend our conscience to our dealing;
The Ten Commandments will not budge
And stealing will continue stealing."

✠   ✠   ✠

Moses, no doubt, had a hard time convincing the Israelites that the Ten Commandments would work.

— *Indianapolis Times*

✠   ✠   ✠

"Well, George," said a country clergyman to an old man who sat by the wayside breaking stones, "that pile doesn't seem to get any less."

"No, vicar," replied the old man, "them stones is like the Ten Commandments. You kin go on breakin' 'em, but you can't get rid of 'em."

Vice

All animals are strictly dry,
    They sinless live and quickly die;
But sinful, gin-ful, rum-soaked men
    Survive for three score years and ten!

✄   ✄   ✄

The country boy goes to the city, marries his employer's daughter, enslaves some hundreds of his fellow humans, gets rich and leaves a public library to his home town.

— Seymour Deming

✄   ✄   ✄

"Father, are all Bolshevists red?"
"No, son, some of them are pretty blue."

— Der Brummer (Berlin)

✄   ✄   ✄

Minister's Wife — "Wake up! There are burglars in the house."

Minister — "Well, what of it? Let them find out their mistake themselves."

— College of the Pacific Weekly

✄   ✄   ✄

No wonder some sinners get so hard-boiled. They are always in hot water.

✄   ✄   ✄

One day at a most inconvenient moment, just as Father Monsabre, the famous preacher of Notre Dame, was preparing to enter the pulpit, a lady came to him with many airs and redundancies, told him that her conscience troubled her greatly, because she had that morning admired herself in the looking glass more than usual, thinking how pretty she was. Whereupon he answered: "Go in peace, my child, a mistake is not a sin."

—The Sign (1921)

✄   ✄   ✄

Corporations have no souls to save and no bodies to kick.

— Richard Coke

✄   ✄   ✄

"It would have proved a striking feature of a vision presented to Adam that day after the death of Abel to have brought before his eyes half a million of men crowded together in the space of a square mile. When the first father had exhausted his wonder in the multitude of his offspring, he would naturally inquire of his angelic instructor for what purpose so vast a multitude had assembled — what is the common end? Alas! to murder each other; all Cains and no Abels!"

✄   ✄   ✄

In a speech in London delivered in 1878 Benjamin Disraeli had this to say of Gladstone, "He is a sophisticated rhetorician, inebriated with the exuberance of his own verbosity, and gifted with an egotistical imagination that can at all times command an interminable and inconsistent series of arguments to malign an opponent and to glorify himself."

✄   ✄   ✄

An eminent speaker at the Congregationalist meeting in New Jersey, was telling the other day of a Westerner's opinion of the East.

"This man," said the speaker, "was a prominent churchman and had occasion to visit New York, where he remained for a few days. In writing of his experiences to his wife in the West he had this to say: 'New York is a great city, but I do wish I had come here before I was converted.' "

— *Newark Star*

♎   ♎   ♎

A Negro minister discovered two men playing cards on Sunday — and for money. "Rastus," said the minister, "Don' you know it's wrong to play cards on de Sabbath?"

"Yes, pahson," answered Rastus ruefully. "But, believe me, ah's payin' foh mah sins."

— *The Hudsonian*

♎   ♎   ♎

The pastor was examining one of the younger classes, and asked the question: "What are the sins of omission?" After a little silence one young lady offered:

"Please, sir, they're sins we ought to have committed, and haven't."

♎   ♎   ♎

"A little stealing is a dangerous part,
   But stealing largely is a noble art,
'Tis mean to rob a hen-roost of a hen,
   But stealing millions makes us gentlemen."

♎   ♎   ♎

A Negro preacher in a Georgia town was edified on one occasion by the recital of a dream had by a member of his church.

"I was dreamin' all dis time," said the narrator, "dat I was in Ole Satan's dominions. I tell you, pahson, dat was shore a bad dream!"

"Was there any white men dere?" asked the dusky divine.

"Shore dere was — plenty of 'em," the other hastened to assure his minister.

"What was dey a-doin'?"

"Ebbery one of 'em," was the answer, "was holding a colored person over a red-hot fire."

Vicar — "I want to speak to you about the milk you are delivering here, Jennings. We don't require it for christenings."

✄   ✄   ✄

"I found a tribe in Africa," said the explorer, "that had absolutely no idea of morality or immorality."

"That's interesting," said the mild lunatic, "but what did they do for plays?"

— *Puck*

✄   ✄   ✄

"I never knew till I got a car," said Brother Jonathan, "that profanity was so prevalent."

"Do you hear much of it on the road?"

"Why," said Brother Jonathan, "nearly everyone that I bump into swears dreadfully."

— *Philadelphia Inquirer*

✄   ✄   ✄

The hard part is to love your neighbor as your pelf.

✄   ✄   ✄

"I want your advice, Mr. Prosie," said the churchwarden to the vicar.

"Yes, dear friend," replied the reverend gentleman; "and on what subject?"

"I've taken to playing golf," explained the other, "and I — er — I find it difficult to restrain — er —"

"Ah, I see what you mean," said the vicar; "bad language."

"Exactly," replied the pillar of the church.

"Well, how would it be to put a stone in your pocket every time you found yourself using wrong words, just as a reminder, you know?"

"The very thing," exclaimed the church warden. "Thank you so much!" And so they parted.

A few days later the worthy cleric was passing along the road which led to the links, when he met an individual whose clothes stuck out all over with great knobby lumps.

"Gracious me, Mr. Bagshawe," he cried, as the object approached nearer, "is that really you?"

"Yes, it's me," grunted the voice of his warden.

"Why, you don't mean — surely all those are not the result of my suggestion?" continued the horrified parson, gazing at the telltale bulges.

"These!" snorted the other, contemptuously; "why these are only the 'dashits.' The others are coming along on a wheelbarrow."

— London Tid-Bits

A Negro preacher concluded his sermon on wisdom with the following, "It ain't the things you don't know what gets you into trouble, it's the things you know for sure that ain't so."

Still Ananias would have his good points as a caddie.

— Shreveport Journal

In a bookstore window appears the legend: "What's Wrong With The World? G. K. Chesterton." Hardened cynics will fear, however, that there is more than that the matter with it.

The most discouraging fact is not that prisons are so overcrowded, but that they ought to be more so.

— Ohio State Journal

Pleasant it is for the Little Tin Gods
    When Great Jove nods.
But the Little Tin Gods make their mistakes,
    That they miss the hour when the Great Jove wakes.

The vicar awarding prizes at a dog show was scandalized by the costumes worn by members of the fairer sex.

"Now look at that youngster," said he, "the one with the cropped hair, the cigarette, and breeches, holding the two pups. Is it a boy or girl?"

"A girl," said his companion, "she's my daughter."

The vicar was flustered — "Do forgive me. I would never have been so outspoken had I known you were her father."

"I'm not her father. I'm her mother."

        �ം   ✱   ✱

They tell a story about Cal Coolidge returning home from church and his wife asked him what the sermon was about.

"Sin," said the President.

"What did he say about it?"

"He was against it."

        ✱   ✱   ✱

LITTLE PILGRIMS

We are weary little pilgrims, straying in a world of gloom. Just behind us is the cradle, just before us is the tomb; there is nothing much to guide us, or the proper path to mark, as we toddle on our journey, little pilgrims in the dark. And we jostle, and we struggle in our feeble, futile wrath, always striving, always reaching to push others from the path; and the wrangling and the jangling of our peevish voices rise, to the seraphim that watch us through the starholes in the skies; and they say, "The foolish pilgrims! Watch them as they push and shove! They might have a pleasant ramble, if their hearts were full of love, if they'd cheer and help each other from the hour that they embark — but they are only blind and erring little pilgrims in the dark."

— Walt Mason

Virtue

The priest was consoling the old lady who had many troubles but who had made a habit of looking at the bright side of things.

"I'm pleased to see Mrs. Hoskins," he said, "that all your misfortunes have not soured you, that you are still grateful to the Almighty."

"Oh, yes, I'm still grateful. My rheumatiz is very bad, but I thank Heaven that I still have a back to have it in."

❈   ❈   ❈

Blessed are the peacemakers. Nobody erects hideous bronze statues to them.

❈   ❈   ❈

Lady — "They say Father Hooley advanced to the attack with a prayer book in one hand and a bomb in the other."

Returned Soldier — "They're always thryin t' belittle, mum."

Lady — "Why, isn't it true?"

Soldier — "No, lady, he had bombs in both hands."

— Life

❈   ❈   ❈

"As a candle white
In a holy place
So is the beauty
Of an aged face."

❈   ❈   ❈

"Once," said the Persian poet Sadi, "I murmured at the vicissitudes of fortune when my feet were bare, and I had not the means of procuring shoes. I entered the mosque with a heavy heart, and there beheld a man deprived of his feet. I offered up my praise and thanksgiving to heaven for its bounty, and bore with patience the want of shoes."

❊ ❊ ❊

Among the souvenirs in the Mark Twain Memorial in Hartford, Conn., one finds these words written on white paper and neatly framed:

Always do right. It will gratify some people and astonish the rest. Truly yours, Mark Twain, New York, Feb. 16, 1901.

❊ ❊ ❊

ST. ZITA

Z for St. Zita, the good kitchen-maid;
She prayed, and she prayed, and she prayed and she prayed:
One morning she got so absorbed in her prayers
She simply neglected her household affairs.
Too late she remembered, 'twas bread-making day,
And she trembled to think what her mistress would say.
She flew to the oven, looked in it and cried;
"Glory be to the Lord! the bread's ready inside."
The Angels had kneaded it, raised it with yeast,
Made the fire, put the pans in the oven — at least.
I can only suppose that is how it was done,
For the bread was all baked by a quarter to one.
To pray like St. Zita, but not to be late,
Is the way to be good (and if possible) great.

— Rev. H. Benson

❊ ❊ ❊

One of the good friends of President Hoover suggested the following bit of verse to be framed and hung in the fishing lodge of the chief executive:

Lord, suffer me to catch a fish so large that even I
In talking of it afterwards shall have no need to lie

To err is human; to admit it is not.

— *Florence Herald* (Ala.)

❋ ❋ ❋

No man e'er felt the halter draw
With good conception of the law.

— *John Trumbull*

❋ ❋ ❋

Sunday-School Teacher (*giving moral lesson to class*) — "And what qualities should you ask God to give you as you grow up? Truth, Honesty, and what else?"
Wise Child — "Sales Resistance."

❋ ❋ ❋

"Have you said your prayers?" asked Willie's mother.
"Of course!" replied the child.
"And did you ask to be made a better little boy?"
"Yes, and I put in a word for you and father, too."

— *London Tid-Bits*

❋ ❋ ❋

The humblest citizen in all the land when clad in the armor of a righteous cause is stronger than the whole hosts of error they can bring.

— *Wm. J. Bryan*

❋ ❋ ❋

"Though thou be born in a hovel, if thou hast virtue, thou art like the lotus growing from the slime!"

— *Buddhist Proverb*

❋ ❋ ❋

The Chinaman pays all his debts when, according to the calendar, the New Year comes around. The American pays $10 or $15 cover charge and gets deeper in.

— *Washington Star*

St. Peter — "I see that you were a bank cashier the greater part of your life."

Banker — "Yes, I was cashier and president of a small town bank."

St. Peter — "How much did you steal?"

Banker — "Nothing."

St. Peter — "How much money was placed in your care during that time?"

Banker — "Millions."

St. Peter — "How much were you paid a year?"

Banker — "About five thousand."

St. Peter — "Here. Take my place."

ӿ   ӿ   ӿ

When in doubt, tell the truth.

— Mark Twain

ӿ   ӿ   ӿ

To right his wrongs, the Russian appeals to dynamite, the American to rebellion, the Irish to agitation, the Indian to his tomahawk, but the Negro, the most patient, the most unresentful and law-abiding, depends upon his songs, his midnight prayers, and inherent faith in the justice of his cause.

— Booker T. Washington

ӿ   ӿ   ӿ

A long life may not be good enough, but a good life is long enough.

— Benjamin Franklin

ӿ   ӿ   ӿ

Live in such a manner that you won't be afraid to sell your parrot to the town's worst gossip.

ӿ   ӿ   ӿ

Lightning-Bug Piety — Bright for a while and soon out.

Idleness — Busy souls have no time to be busybodies.

— *O'Malley*

✄   ✄   ✄

People who stay away from church may be sent away from the Pearly Gate.

✄   ✄   ✄

"Blessed are the peacemakers." They never have to worry about unemployment.

— *Kenosha News* (Wis.)

✄   ✄   ✄

So live that when your summons comes you won't have to burn the books.

— *Stockton Independent*

✄   ✄   ✄

The laborer is worthy of his hire — if his labor is.

— *Wall Street Journal*

✄   ✄   ✄

Man wants little here below but he usually gets along on less.

— *Little Rock Gazette* (Ark.)

✄   ✄   ✄

"Bert," said Hennessey, "we ought to like our neighbors as we like ourselves."

"Well," said Dooley, "maybe we ought to like them better. We know less about them."

✄   ✄   ✄

A lady was once talking with an archbishop upon the subject of juvenile education, and ended by saying:

"Well, your Grace, I have made up my mind never to put my child under religious education until he has arrived at the years of discretion."

"Well, I can assure you that if you neglect him all that time that the devil will not."

The adage that "the good die young" originated in the observation that we meet so few of them in the adult stage.

— *Columbia Record*

※ ※ ※

St. Thomas More going to Tower Hill for his execution said to the officer accompanying him, "I pray thee, see me safely up, as for my coming down I can shift for myself. Pluck up thy spirits, my neck is very short."

The saint seemed to speak in jest as he moved his beard from the block, with the remark that it had never committed treason.

※ ※ ※

Brother Juan de la Misceria painted the portrait of St. Theresa of Avila. Brother Juan was a phenomenon which every religious order seems to produce, both before his time and since; I mean he had a "a talent for art," or thought he had, or was supposed by others to have, and insisted upon displaying it. And when poor St. Theresa gazed upon Brother Juan's production, she said, "May God forgive him for making me so ugly!" And the exclamation is priceless. In it we read the woman in the saint, and all her books are nothing other than that — the marvelous exposition of the progress of a most human and passionate soul through all the dangers and difficulties of human life, upward to the peaks of an almost unexampled sanctity.

— *Michael Williams* in *America*

※ ※ ※

When Professor Wendell of Harvard entered upon his Sabbatical year, he remained in Cambridge some weeks after his leave of absence began and persisted in taking part in the departmental meeting. The head of the department protested.

"Sir," he said, "you are officially absent, you are *non est.*"

"Oh, very well," replied Professor Wendell, "a *non est* man is the noblest work of God."

— *Success*

Sunday-School Teacher — "Now, Jimmy, I want you to memorize today's motto, 'It is more blessed to give than to receive.' "

Jimmy — "Yes'm, but I know it now. My father says he has always used that as his motto in business."

Teacher — "Oh, how noble of him! And what is his business?"

Jimmy — "He's a prize fighter, ma'am."

— Life

        ✄   ✄   ✄

The immortal Dante tells us that divine justice weighs the sins of the cold-blooded and the sins of the warm-blooded in different scales.

— Franklin Delano Roosevelt

        ✄   ✄   ✄

Two ministers were driving in a cab to the station. Anxious lest they miss their train, one of them took out his watch and found it had stopped.

"How annoying, I always put such faith in that watch."

"In a case like that," said the other, "I think good works would be better."

        ✄   ✄   ✄

It was in an assembly, one of the speakers going to tell a shady story, asked, "Are there any ladies present?" looking around suspiciously.

To which General Grant curtly replied, "No, but there are gentlemen present."

        ✄   ✄   ✄

Legion of Decency's cable to Gandhi, "Keep Your Shirt On."

— Catholic Daily Tribune

Wills

In a legal transaction involving the title to a parcel of land in Louisiana a firm of New York attorneys handling the matter requested that a title opinion be furnished. A New Orleans lawyer who was retained to check the title rendered an opinion tracing the title back to 1803. The New York attorneys examined the opinion and wrote again to the New Orleans lawyer, saying in effect, that the opinion rendered was all very well as far as it went, but the title to the property prior to 1803 had not been satisfactorily covered. The southern attorney replied as follows:

Dear Sirs:

I am in receipt of your favor of the fifth inst., inquiring as to the state of the title prior to the year 1803.

Please be advised that in the year 1803 the United States of America acquired the territory of Louisiana by purchase from France. The Republic of France, in turn, acquired title from the Spanish Crown, by conquest. The Spanish Crown having originally acquired title by virtue of the discoveries of one Christopher Columbus, a Genoese sailor who had been duly authorized to embark on his voyage of discovery by Isabella, Queen of Spain. Isabella, before granting such authority had obtained the sanction of his holiness, the Pope. The Pope is vicar of Christ on earth. Christ is Son of God. God made Louisiana.

Very truly yours,

✠   ✠   ✠

What about the following will as a characteristic of our up-to-date American morals?

To my wife, I leave her lover and the knowledge that I wasn't the fool she thought I was.

To my son, I leave the pleasure of earning a living. For thirty-five years he has thought that the pleasure was all mine. He was mistaken.

To my daughter, I leave $100,000. She will need it. The only good piece of business her husband ever did was to marry her.

To my valet, I leave the clothes that he has been stealing from me regularly for the past ten years. Also, my fur coat that he wore last winter while I was at Palm Beach.

To my chauffeur, I leave my cars. He almost ruined them, and I want him to have the fun of finishing the job.

To my partner, I leave the suggestion that he take some other clever man in with him at once if he expects to do any business.

※   ※   ※

Better leave yure children virtew, than money, but this is a sekret known only to a few.   — *Josh Billings*

※   ※   ※

Where there's a will there are disappointed relatives.

※   ※   ※

The following address was made to the people of Springfield, Ill., by Abraham Lincoln on departing for Washington to assume the presidency:

"My friends, no one not in my position can realize the sadness I feel at this parting. To this people I owe all that I am. Here I have lived more than a quarter of a century. Here my children were born, and here one of them lies buried. I know not how soon I shall see you again. I go to assume a task more than that which has devolved upon any other man since the days of Washington. He never would have succeeded except for the aid of Divine Providence, upon which he at all times relied. I feel that I cannot succeed without the same Divine blessing which sustained him, and on the same Almighty Being I place my reliance for support. And I hope you, my friends, will all pray that I may receive that Divine assistance without which I cannot succeed, but with which a success is certain. Again, I bid you an affectionate farewell."